U.S. Government

Grades 5-8

by
Ron Wheeler

Published by Instructional Fair
an imprint of
Frank Schaffer Publications®

Instructional Fair

Author: Ron Wheeler
Cover Artist: Matthew Van Zomeren
Interior Artist: Don Ellens
Photo Credits: © Digital Stock

Frank Schaffer Publications®

Instructional Fair is an imprint of Frank Schaffer Publications.

Send all inquiries to:
Frank Schaffer Publications
3195 Wilson Drive NW
Grand Rapids, Michigan 49534

U.S. Government—grades 5–8

ISBN: 0-7424-0055-7

5 6 7 8 9 10 11 PAT 10 09 08 07 06 05

Introduction

American democracy cannot function without informed and active citizens. This book will help your students develop an awareness and better understanding of our democratic system and introduce them to the political process through a variety of engaging activities.

The first section of *U.S. Government* focuses on topics suggested for grades 5-8 in the national standards for civics and government. These topics, in the form of questions, include the following: What is the purpose of government? What is the American political system? How does the government established by the Constitution reflect the principles of American democracy? What is the relationship of the United States to other nations and to world affairs? What are the roles of the citizen in American democracy?

Specifically, there are activities on understanding and analyzing the following topics:
- the Declaration of Independence
- the U.S. Constitution and Amendments
- the federal system of government
- the levels of government
- the branches of government
- limited and unlimited government
- the separation of powers
- the system of checks and balances
- the rights and responsibilities of citizenship
- the ideals and values of American democracy
- comparative governments and international relations
- participation in a democracy

The presidents of the United States are the focus in the remaining section of the book. Biographical information about each of the U.S. presidents is presented in a unique "President Card" format. Also included is a time line that highlights significant events that occurred during each president's administration. Activities for student use of the president cards and presidential time line begin on page 79. These cards and time line can be used in a variety of ways. They can be used to aid in the study of information about the presidents, as a tool for practicing chronology, as an aid in working on classification and comparison skills, and as a basis of individual, team, and classroom games.

Introducing your students to the challenging activities found in this book may well increase the probability that they will want to get involved in the political life of their community, state, and nation.

Table of Contents

Symbols of Our Nation

The United States has many symbols associated with it as a nation. They include objects, songs, documents, poems, places, and events. On the right below is a list of American symbols. On the left are words and phrases related to the symbols. Your task is to match the two by writing the correct letter on the blank in front of the number.

Words and Phrases

____ 1. "Give me your tired, your poor . . ."

____ 2. "Proclaim liberty throughout all the land . . ."

____ 3. "O'er the land of the free and the home of the brave"

____ 4. Old Glory

____ 5. "In God We Trust"

____ 6. *E pluribus unum* (one out of many)

____ 7. "I . . . will . . . preserve, protect, and defend the Constitution of the United States."

____ 8. ". . . with liberty and justice for all"

____ 9. I believe in the United States of America as a government of the people, by the people, for the people . . ."

____ 10. "Let freedom ring!"

Symbols

A. America (My Country 'Tis of Thee)

B. The Great Seal of the United States

C. National Motto

D. The Flag of the United States

E. Statue of Liberty

F. Liberty Bell

G. The American's Creed

H. Presidential Oath of Office

I. Pledge of Allegiance to the Flag

J. National Anthem

What's It For?

Government is the people and institutions empowered to make decisions about laws and how they are carried out. Laws deal with many issues and problems including how resources are distributed, how revenues are collected, and how conflicts are resolved. Below is a list of ideas about the purposes government should serve. Your task is to rank each idea from "1" for the most important or most acceptable purpose to "10" for the least important or most unacceptable purpose. Write the reasons for your ranking on the lines provided.

Rank	Reason
____ Protecting the rights of individuals	_____
____ Providing economic security	_____
____ Promoting the general welfare	_____
____ Molding the character of citizens	_____
____ Furthering the interests of a particular group	_____
____ Promoting a particular religion	_____
____ Providing military security	_____
____ Establishing moral principles	_____
____ Promoting a particular political party	_____
____ Promoting the spread of information	_____

In Your Own Words

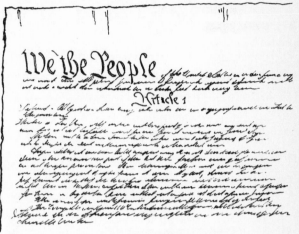

The Preamble to the Constitution of the United States is presented below. After you read the preamble, identify the six purposes of government stated in it. Then, tell what each of these purposes means in your own words.

We the People of the United States, in Order to form a more perfect Union, establish Justice, insure domestic Tranquility, provide for the common defense, promote the general Welfare, and secure the Blessings of Liberty to ourselves and our Posterity, do ordain and establish this Constitution for the United States of America.

The purposes of government, as stated in the Preamble to the Constitution, are to

1. _____

   In your own words this means _____

2. _____

   In your own words this means _____

3. _____

   In your own words this means _____

4. _____

   In your own words this means _____

5. _____

   In your own words this means _____

6. _____

   In your own words this means _____

Functions of Government

Some functions of government are listed below inside the boxes. For each of the purposes, write down on a separate sheet of paper a specific example of how it affects you or someone you know personally.

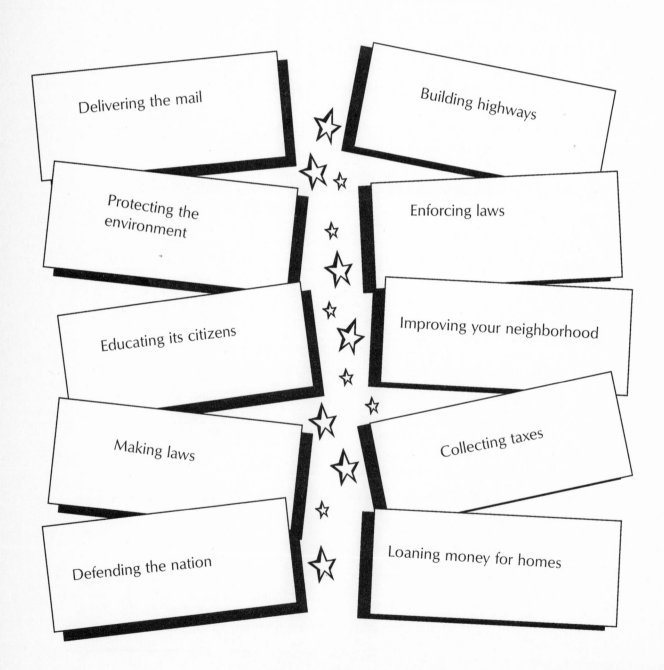

Delivering the mail

Building highways

Protecting the environment

Enforcing laws

Educating its citizens

Improving your neighborhood

Making laws

Collecting taxes

Defending the nation

Loaning money for homes

Steps Toward Revolution

A series of events led to the start of the Revolutionary War and the writing of the Declaration of Independence. Many of these events are presented in random order below. Your task is to investigate each event, and then place it in correct chronological order on the time line along the bottom of the page. Place the letter inside the appropriate box along the time line.

A. British close Boston Harbor, which prompts the First Continental Congress to stop trade with Britain.

B. British soldiers kill five colonists in the Boston Massacre, which increases colonies' anti-British feelings.

C. British Parliament passes the Declaratory Act, which proclaims Parliament's right to make laws for the American colonies without their consent.

D. King George issues a Proclamation which forbids colonists from settling all lands west of the Appalachian Mountains.

E. British Parliament passes the Sugar Act, which taxes molasses and sugar imported to the colonies.

F. British soldiers and colonial militia fight at Lexington and Concord.

G. British Parliament passes the Stamp Act, which taxes all official documents.

H. British Parliament passes the Tea Act, which taxes tea.

I. Colonists form "Committees of Correspondence" to increase communication among the colonies.

□	□	□	□	□	□	□	□	□
1763	1764	1765	1766	1770	1772	1773	1774	1775

Declaration of Independence

The Declaration of Independence was written after the start of the Revolutionary War. It declared America's freedom from British rule. The Second Continental Congress appointed five men—Thomas Jefferson, John Adams, Benjamin Franklin, Robert Livingston, and Robert Sherman—to write it. Jefferson wrote the first draft, which was almost perfect. The committee made a few corrections before it was presented to the Continental Congress. A few corrections were made, but the document is basically the work of Jefferson. Church bells rang to signal the adoption of the Declaration of Independence on July 4, 1776—the birth of our nation. Some important statements from the Declaration of Independence are presented below. On the lines under each statement or phrase, write down what the statement means in your own words.

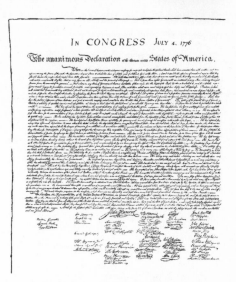

"When in the course of human events it becomes necessary for one people to dissolve the political bands which have connected them with another . . ."

_____

_____

_____

"We hold these truths to be self-evident, that all men are created equal . . . [and have the rights of] life, liberty, and the pursuit of happiness . . ."

_____

_____

_____

"The history of the present King of Great Britain is a history of repeated injuries and usurpations, all having in direct object the establishment of an absolute tyranny over these states . . ."

_____

_____

_____

Framers of the Constitution

After you read about the Framers of the Constitution, answer the questions that follow. How did the 55 delegates who met in the summer of 1787 in Philadelphia get the title "Framers of the Constitution" and a prominent place in the history books? Before the Philadelphia meeting, the national government, under the Articles of Confederation, was too weak to rule effectively. Because of this, many people were angry and demanded changes. The delegates originally came to Philadelphia to deal with these problems and make recommendations for changes. However, they quickly made the bold decision to write a completely new constitution for the country. The Constitution they wrote, or framed, is the one we have today. It begins with these words: "We the People of the United States, in Order to form a more perfect Union, . . ."

The delegates to the meeting, or *Constitutional Convention* as it is now called, included some of the most famous names in American history. George Washington was elected president of the convention. Many of the delegates were only in their 30s, including James Madison and Alexander Hamilton. The oldest delegate was Benjamin Franklin at 81. James Madison is credited with contributing more to the writing of the Constitution than any of the others, which earned him the title "Father of the Constitution." Over half of the framers were lawyers and judges, a fourth were landowners, all of them had held at least one public office, and all of them were wealthy.

Though the framers differed on many issues, they were a daring and creative group, who were willing to take steps to establish a strong national government. Throughout the summer, the framers debated, wrote, and rewrote the Constitution. Finally, on September 17, 1787, the framers finished their work. The new Constitution proposed a powerful executive and a Senate with powers equal to those of the House of Representatives. Now it was up to the states to accept or reject the Constitution.

1. In what city did the delegates meet? _____
2. How many delegates came to the meeting? _____
3. What kinds of backgrounds did the delegates have? _____
4. Why did the delegates meet? _____
5. Did they have an easy job to do? _____
6. Who was the oldest delegate? _____
7. Who was elected president of the meeting? _____
8. What was the meeting called? _____
9. Who was called the "Father of the Constitution"? _____
10. What was the main difference between the Articles of Confederation and the Constitution? _____

The Constitutional Convention

There were several areas of disagreement at the Constitutional Convention in 1787. The greatest concern was in deciding how many representatives from each state should be in the legislature. Three plans were devised to solve the problem. They were as follows:

The Virginia Plan—This proposal called for a bicameral, or two-house, legislature with states with larger populations having more representatives than states with smaller populations.

The New Jersey Plan—This proposal called for a unicameral, or single-chamber, legislature with all states having an equal number of representatives.

The Connecticut Plan—This proposal called for a bicameral, or two-house legislature. One, the Senate, would have an equal number of members. The other, the House of Representatives, would have a representative for every 30,000 residents. This plan satisfied both the large and small states and became known as the Great Compromise.

1. Imagine that you are a delegate to the convention from a state with a small population. Write a brief statement about which plan you would probably favor, and why.

   _____

   _____

   _____

2. Next, imagine you are a delegate from a state with a large population. Write a statement about which plan you would probably favor, and why.

   _____

   _____

   _____

3. Finally, write why you might be persuaded to compromise on this issue. If you did, which plan would you vote for?

   _____

   _____

Powerful Ideas

When the Framers of the Constitution assembled in Philadelphia in 1787, they dealt with some very powerful ideas, which are listed in the column on the right. Match the ideas with their correct definitions, which are presented in the left column. Write the letter on the line in front of the number.

Definitions

____ 1. a proposal for a two-house legislation with representatives in both houses based on each state's population

____ 2. government by the people

____ 3. a government regulated by a written or unwritten statement of principles and functions

____ 4. division of governmental powers between the legislative, executive, and judicial branches

____ 5. a proposal for a two-house legislature that gave equal representation to one house (Senate) and representation based on population in the other house (House of Representatives)

____ 6. a two-house form of government

____ 7. a proposal for a single-house form of legislature with equal representation

____ 8. a government in which citizens elect officials to represent them

____ 9. a government in which power is divided between states and a central authority

____10. a division of governmental powers in which each branch has some control and influence over the power of the others

Powerful Idea

A. Republic

B. Separation of Power

C. New Jersey Plan

D. Connecticut Plan

E. Virginia Plan

F. Federalism

G. Democracy

H. Bicameralism

I. Constitutional Government

J. Checks and Balances

Outlining the Constitution

The United States Constitution is a marvelous document. It has guided our nation for over 200 years. You will need a copy of the Constitution to fill in the outline below. Write a few key words on each line to briefly identify each article, section, and the Bill of Rights.
Preamble: We the people . . .

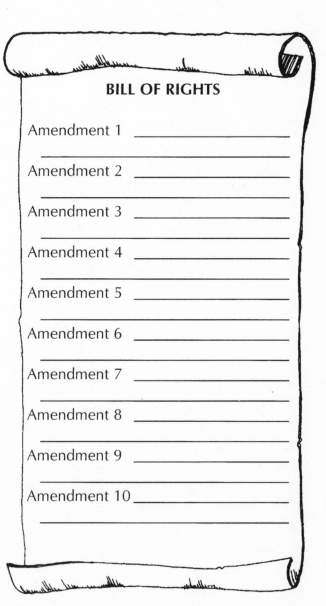

Article I _____
Section 1 _____
Section 2 _____
Section 3 _____
Section 4 _____
Section 5 _____
Section 6 _____
Section 7 _____
Section 8 _____
Section 9 _____
Section 10 _____
Article II _____
Section 1 _____
Section 2 _____
Section 3 _____
Section 4 _____
Article III _____
Section 1 _____
Section 2 _____
Section 3 _____
Article IV _____
Section 1 _____
Section 2 _____
Section 3 _____
Section 4 _____
Article V _____
Article VI _____
Section 1 _____
Section 2 _____
Section 3 _____
Article VII _____

BILL OF RIGHTS

Amendment 1 _____
_____
Amendment 2 _____
_____
Amendment 3 _____
_____
Amendment 4 _____
_____
Amendment 5 _____
_____
Amendment 6 _____
_____
Amendment 7 _____
_____
Amendment 8 _____
_____
Amendment 9 _____
_____
Amendment 10 _____
_____

Amendment Matchup

Nothing is perfect, not even the U.S. Constitution. Over time, the needs and circumstances of a society change. The Framers of the Constitution realized this when they provided for changes in the Constitution. Amendments to the Constitution have either been additions to or changes in the original document. Since the Bill of Rights was added to the Constitution in 1791, only 17 amendments have been ratified. Listed below on the right are the amendments and the dates they became part of the Constitution. On the left are statements that describe what the amendments are about. Consult a copy of the amendment section of the Constitution to determine what each amendment is about. Then write the amendment's number on the line in front of the statement describing it.

Statements

_____ A. Repealed the Eighteenth Amendment

_____ B. Described the rights of citizens, representation, and voting

_____ C. Stated no one could be kept from voting for not paying taxes

_____ D. Did away with slavery

_____ E. Gave vote to citizens aged 18 and older

_____ F. Gave women the right to vote

_____ G. Stated that no person can be elected president more than twice

_____ H. Allowed voters to elect senators

_____ I. Provided for succession to the presidency and presidential disability

_____ J. Stated that no one could be denied the vote because of race, color, or because he was a former slave

_____ K. Changed the dates of the president and vice president's term in office

_____ L. Prohibited the manufacture and sale of liquor

_____ M. Gave citizens who live in Washington, D.C., the right to vote in presidential elections

_____ N. Explained what kinds of cases federal courts could try

_____ O. Changed how the electoral college voted

_____ P. Stated that laws passed to increase the salaries of senators and representatives could not take effect until after an election of representatives had taken place

_____ Q. Gave Congress the power to collect taxes on income

Amendments

Amendment 11 (1795)
Amendment 12 (1804)
Amendment 13 (1865)
Amendment 14 (1868)
Amendment 15 (1870)
Amendment 16 (1913)
Amendment 17 (1913)
Amendment 18 (1919)
Amendment 19 (1920)
Amendment 20 (1933)
Amendment 21 (1933)
Amendment 22 (1951)
Amendment 23 (1961)
Amendment 24 (1964)
Amendment 25 (1967)
Amendment 26 (1971)
Amendment 27 (1992)

Constitution Fill-In

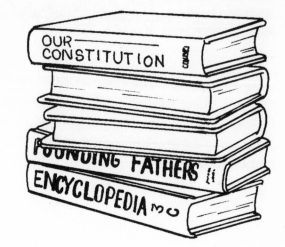

Use classroom and library resources to find the correct words to write on the blanks.

1. All of the original 13 states attended the Constitutional Convention except _____.

2. A total of _____ states had to approve the Constitution to make it "the law of the land."

3. The Constitution replaced the Articles of _____.

4. The _____ can veto a bill.

5. _____ is considered the "Father of the Constitution."

6. The body of Congress that can impeach the president is the _____.

7. The body of Congress that has the power to try impeachments is the _____.

8. The branch of government that enforces the laws is the _____.

9. _____ is the city where the Constitutional Convention was held.

10. The president of the Constitutional Convention was _____.

11. The _____ amendment to the Constitution guarantees free speech.

12. The Nineteenth Amendment gave _____ the right to vote.

13. The branch of government that determines whether or not laws are constitutional is the _____.

The Civil Rights Amendments

To solve the crossword puzzle, you will need to know all of the information that follows.

Amendments 13, 14, and 15 are often called the Civil Rights Amendments because they clarified the rights of former slaves after the Civil War. When the Constitution was written, the framers did not mention "slavery" by name. Instead, they referred to all nonslaves except Indians as "free persons" and to slaves as "all other persons." Amendment 13, ratified in 1865, abolishes slavery from the land. It proclaims that "neither slavery nor involuntary servitude . . . shall exist within the United States." Amendment 14, ratified in 1868, made black people citizens and entitled them to the same rights guaranteed all citizens by the Constitution. Amendment 15, ratified in 1870, spells out that "the right of citizens of the United States to vote shall not be denied . . . by the United States or by any state on account of race, color, or previous condition of servitude [slavery]." (Until 1920 only adult male citizens had the Constitutional right to vote.) Despite the Civil Rights Amendments, the principles of freedom and equality would continue to elude black Americans for another hundred years. The civil rights movement, which emerged in the 1950s and 1960s, helped make these principles a reality in America, but the battle against racism continues to this day.

Across

3. Amendment 13 held out this promise for blacks.
6. Amendments 13, 14, and 15 are often called _____ amendments.
7. Thanks to the Civil Rights Amendments, blacks were entitled to _____ treatment under the law.

Down

1. This amendment made blacks citizens.
2. What word was not mentioned in the Constitution?
4. No citizen can be kept from voting because of this.
5. What war was fought between the states?

Financing Government

The U.S. Constitution sets forth how the American people will pay for government. It is through taxation. Sections 7 and 8 of Article I identify provisions that give Congress the "power to lay and collect taxes." For a long time, the only way Congress got money to pay debts and provide the necessary defense for the country was through taxing imported items, and on items made, sold, and used in the United States. This changed in 1913 when the Sixteenth Amendment was added to the Constitution. The Sixteenth Amendment gives Congress the specific right to tax individuals according to the amount of income they earn. Everyone agrees that an income tax ought to be fair, but fewer people agree on how this should be done. In fact, more people probably complain more about the income tax than any other government policy.

1. Do you think the Sixteenth Amendment, which allows the government to tax incomes, is a fair one? Explain your answer.

2. Think of some ways the government spends the money received from individuals' incomes. List them here.

3. Why do you think people complain about the Sixteenth Amendment?

Take a poll. Ask some people if they think paying an income tax is necessary, if it is fair, and if they can suggest other ways for the government to raise money.

Person	Necessary?	Fair?	Other Ways?
1			
2			
3			
4			

The Twenty-Sixth Amendment

In 1971 the Twenty-sixth Amendment gave 18-year-olds the right to vote. At the time, it was believed that young voters would have a major impact on American politics. But this has not been the case. Instead, voter turnout among 18- to 24-year-old citizens is the lowest of any age group. The turnout of below 20% for the 1998 midterm election was perhaps the lowest ever. These are troubling findings when you consider that the 70.2 million American youth who are younger than 18 comprise the largest generation of young people in our nation's history.

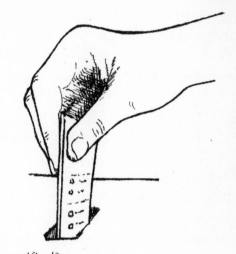

1. Why do you think the Twenty-sixth Amendment was ratified?

   _____

   _____

   _____

2. Why is the voter turnout among 18- to 24-year-olds so low?

   _____

   _____

   _____

3. Do you think the Twenty-sixth Amendment should be repealed?

   _____

   _____

   _____

4. Take a survey. Ask several students if they think 18- to 24-year-olds should vote. Can they suggest reasons why this age group ranks lowest? Record your answers below.

   Student #1

   Student #2

   Student #3

Amending the Constitution

The Constitution has been a lasting document. Written over 200 years ago, its authors realized times would change so they provided a way the Constitution could be changed when necessary.

1. Which article provides for such changes?

   _____

2. What is a change in the Constitution called?

   _____

Scott Farnum
74 Fourth Avenue
Grand Isle, Maine 04746

The Honorable John W Smith
United States Senate
Washington, D.C. 20015

Dear Senator Smith:

It Has been brought to my attention that this will cost those in the low lands to be Washington is not the place to force the is thereof a please reconsider your dis· Pleas · consider standing with us

Very truly yours
Scott Farnum

A change to the Constitution may be proposed when either two thirds of Congress or two thirds of the states request it. To be accepted as part of the Constitution, the proposed amendment must be ratified by three fourths of the states. It is not easy to make constitutional changes. Over 9,000 amendments have been proposed over the years, but only 27 have been ratified by three fourths of the states. Even with popular support from the population at large, such as the Equal Rights Amendment recently had, ratification is not always ensured. Three suggestions for constitutional reform are listed below:

1. Change treaty ratification from two-thirds approval by the Senate to 60 percent.

2. Congress should authorize a limit to campaign spending.

3. Terms for members of the House of Representatives should be four years rather than two.

Citizens-at-large can have input into making changes by writing to their senators and representatives. Select one of the suggestions above. Then write a paragraph expressing your opinion about the suggestion under consideration. Back up your opinions with sound reasoning.

_____

_____

_____

_____

Organization of the U.S. Government

Below is a list of names of various positions, departments, agencies, and groups that operate within the three branches of the United States Government. Your job is to match the name with the correct branch. For each one, place either an E for executive branch, J for judicial branch, or L for legislative branch, on the blank in front of the number.

_____ 1. President

_____ 2. Chief Justice

_____ 3. Speaker

_____ 4. Vice President

_____ 5. Senate

_____ 6. House of Representatives

_____ 7. Supreme Court

_____ 8. White House Office

_____ 9. Cabinet

_____ 10. Courts of Appeals

_____ 11. National Security Council

_____ 12. Library of Congress

_____ 13. General Accounting Office

_____ 14. District Courts

_____ 15. Government Printing Office

_____ 16. Secretary of State

_____ 17. Tax Court

_____ 18. U.S. Botanical Gardens

_____ 19. Sentencing Commission

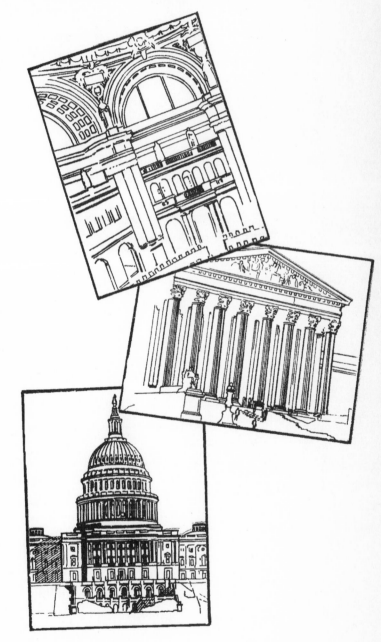

One Nation, Many Governments

Americans live under the jurisdiction of three governments: national, state, and local. Use library resources to identify how powers are separated and shared between the national and state governments. Then, fill in the Venn Diagram below with the appropriate powers.

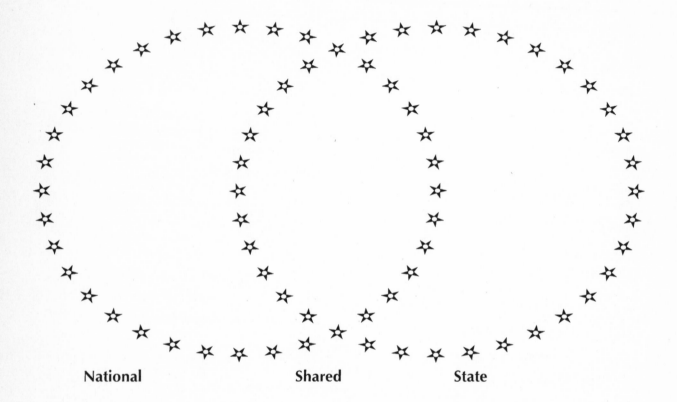

National   **Shared**   **State**

power to tax   law enforcement   borrow money   regulate voting

coin money   raise an army   education   roads

health and hospitals   declare war   conduct foreign relations

Forms of Government

There are different ways to classify governments. With a system to classify governments, you can better compare and analyze them. Read the following two ways to classify governments. Then, answer the questions below.

Confederal, Federal, and Unitary Governments

The relationship between the central government of a nation and other units of government can be classified as confederal, federal, and unitary systems. In a *confederal system* each state is sovereign. This means that each state has the right to rule itself, except for powers delegated to the federal government for specific purposes. Examples of the confederal systems are the United States under the Articles of Confederation and the Confederate States of America. In a federal system, powers are divided and shared between the national and state governments. An example is the government of the United States under the U.S. Constitution. In a unitary system, power is concentrated in the central government. The 50 states and hundreds of local governments which can exercise only those powers given them by central government are examples of unitary systems.

Presidential and Parliamentary Government

Another way to classify governments is based on the relationship between the legislative and executive branches. The United States has a presidential system (also called a system of *shared powers)* in which the powers are separated between the two branches. The president and vice president are chosen by all of the people every four years. Legislators are chosen by people within states and districts. In contrast, in a parliamentary system, such as Great Britain's, the prime minister, who is the chief executive officer, is chosen from among the ranks of the majority party in parliament. (Note: *parliament* is another name for "legislature.")

1. How do presidential and parliamentary governments differ?

   _____

   _____

2. What are the characteristics of confederal, federal, and unitary governments?

   _____

   _____

   _____

A Federal System

The U.S. Constitution created a federal government—a system that divided powers between the national government and the state governments. In some areas, the national government had control, and in other areas, each of the 50 states had control. For each of the powers listed below, write N on the blank if it is controlled by the national government and S on the blank if it is controlled by the state governments. Consult a copy of the U.S. Constitution in a resource book to make certain your answers are correct.

_____ 1. War is declared.

_____ 2. A tax is placed on goods coming into the United States from foreign countries.

_____ 3. Money is provided to repair state roads.

_____ 4. A treaty is made between the United States and another country.

_____ 5. A new stamp is designed.

_____ 6. Speed limits on rural roads are established.

_____ 7. A child must be a certain age before entering school.

_____ 8. The election date for state officials is set.

_____ 9. Money is allotted to build a new aircraft carrier for the U.S. Navy.

_____ 10. Money is printed.

_____ 11. Rules are established for becoming a U.S. citizen.

_____ 12. A license is issued to drive an automobile.

_____ 13. A post office is built in a town.

_____ 14. A person is fined for running a red light.

_____ 15. Salaries for the president and vice president are raised.

_____ 16. Children must attend school until they reach a certain age.

_____ 17. The number of immigrants allowed to come to the United States is increased.

_____ 18. A person goes to trial for spying on the U.S. Government.

Branches of Government

The powers of the national government are distributed among the legislative, executive, and judicial branches. Use library resources to identify the power of each of the three branches. List the powers below inside the appropriate box.

LEGISLATIVE BRANCH

EXECUTIVE BRANCH

JUDICIAL BRANCH

- impeach the president
- nominate members of the federal judiciary
- pass laws over the president's veto by two-thirds majority vote of both Houses
- establish committees to oversee activities of executive branch

- overrule decisions made by lower courts
- disapprove appointments made by the president
- declare laws made by Congress to be unconstitutional

- veto laws passed by Congress
- declare actions of the executive branch to be unconstitutional
- propose amendments to the U.S. Constitution

Checks and Balances Chart

Use classroom and library resources to fill in the chart below. Some boxes will not be filled in.

Power	How It Can Be Checked		
	The President may	The Supreme Court may	Congress may
If Congress passes a law, then . . .			
If the president vetoes a bill passed by Congress, then . . .			
If the president appoints a Supreme Court judge, then . . .			
If a federal judge shows misconduct in office, then . . .			
If the president makes a treaty with another country, then . . .			
If the president enforces an unjust law, then . . .			
If the president asks for money for defense, then . . .			

A Limited and Unlimited Government

The federal, state, and local governments of the United States are characterized by legal limits on their power. The basis for these limits is set forth in the U.S. Constitution and in the state constitutions. They include institutional devices like "checks and balances" and "bill of rights" and "separation of powers." In contrast, governments with unlimited power over their citizens are nonconstitutional governments in which power is in the hands of one person or a small group. A historical example of an unlimited government was Nazi Germany under Adolf Hitler. At the bottom of the page are characteristics of

limited and unlimited governments, as well as historical and contemporary examples of nations with either limited or unlimited governments. Your task is to write the characteristics and examples inside the correct box.

Limited Government	Unlimited Government

Characteristics:
- regular and free elections
- independent judiciaries
- courts controlled by leader
- protection of individual rights
- no restraints on government
- no free elections
- protection from government
- multiple political parties
- laws apply to leaders as well as the governed
- government use of intimidation and terror
- goals and means of government cannot violate constitution

Nations:
Great Britain
Canada
Soviet Union
France
Iraq
Libya
Italy under Mussolini
Myanmar
China

The Executive Branch

The president heads the executive branch of the United States. In Article II of the Constitution, the duties of the president are stated.

1. In Section 1, paragraph 1 of that article it states the length of the president's term. What is it?

   _____

2. Who else is elected at the same time and for the same time period?

   _____

3. What are the three qualifications a person must have to be president?

   _____

   _____

   _____

4. Section 2 of the above Article states what the president's duties are. Place a check mark next to the duties given to the president by the Constitution.

   _____ a. The president may make treaties by himself.

   _____ b. The president appoints the vice president.

   _____ c. The president is commander in chief of the armed forces.

   _____ d. The president makes appointments of ambassadors with the approval of the Senate.

   _____ e. The president sees that federal laws are carried out as they are designed.

   _____ f. The president does not tell Congress what he wants.

   _____ g. The president has the Congress greet visiting ambassadors.

   _____ h. The president may make treaties with the approval of the Senate.

   _____ i. The president commissions officers in the armed forces.

5. On the back of this sheet, write the oath a president must take before entering the presidency—Article II, Section 1, paragraph 8.

Cabinet Officers

The cabinet is an informal group that advises the president. The cabinet consists of the heads of 14 executive departments. The president appoints the heads of the departments, subject to confirmation, or approval, by the Senate. Use a current almanac or other source to identify the current heads of each department. Then write their names on the appropriate blanks below.

Department	Name of Head of Department
1. Secretary of State	_____
2. Secretary of the Treasury	_____
3. Secretary of Defense	_____
4. Attorney General	_____
5. Secretary of the Interior	_____
6. Secretary of Agriculture	_____
7. Secretary of Commerce	_____
8. Secretary of Labor	_____
9. Secretary of Health and Human Services	_____
10. Secretary of Housing and Urban Development	_____
11. Secretary of Transportation	_____
12. Secretary of Energy	_____
13. Secretary of Education	_____
14. Secretary of Veterans Affairs	_____

Getting Elected President

Candidates for the presidency have a long and difficult path to travel before election day. To become the nominee of each major party, a candidate must win delegates to the national convention, which is held in mid-summer. Two imaginary presidential candidates are profiled below. Based upon the information provided, answer the questions below.

Candidate A

Name: Fred Johnson

Profile: age 46, married, three children, war veteran, business person, former senator

Positions: In favor of tax cuts, reducing federal budget, strong military, strong family values, being tough on criminals, and strong state governments.

Against excessive violence on TV and in films.

Candidate B

Name: Barbara North

Profile: age 51, married, one child, lawyer, former governor

Positions: In favor of improving education, federal programs to fight poverty, gun control, strengthening America's role as a world leader, and enhancing civil rights.

Against cutting needed federal programs for needy and prayer in schools.

1. Write a brief description of Candidate A based upon the information provided.

   _____

   _____

   _____

   _____

2. Write a brief description of Candidate B based upon the information provided.

   _____

   _____

   _____

   _____

3. Which candidate do you prefer? _____

   Why? _____

   _____

   _____

   _____

Presidential Power

Every four years the president takes the Oath of Office: "I do solemnly swear [or affirm] that I will faithfully execute the Office of the President of the United States, and will to the best of my Ability, preserve, protect and defend the Constitution of the United States." With the responsibility of running the government comes power which could be misused. The Framers of the Constitution tried to avoid any misuse of presidential power by creating three branches of government—the Legislative, Judicial, and Executive—to check on one another. This system of checks and balances has worked most of the time.

Look at a copy of the Constitution. Use it to help you see how much power the president has been given. Then mark the following statements true or false. Write a "T" or "F" on the blank provided.

_____ 1. The president is the commander in chief of the armed forces.

_____ 2. The president may declare war.

_____ 3. The president has the power to grant reprieves and pardons for offenses against the United States, except in the case of impeachment.

_____ 4. The president has the power to appoint any official to his cabinet, a Supreme Court justice, or an ambassador without approval from Congress.

_____ 5. The War Powers Act was passed so that Congress and the president act together in declaring any act of hostility.

_____ 6. The president is to keep the Congress informed with the State of the Union messages from time to time.

_____ 7. A treaty must receive two-thirds approval from the Senate before it is effective.

_____ 8. The president may recommend legislation.

_____ 9. The president may introduce legislation.

_____ 10. The president may make treaties.

_____ 11. The president must see that the laws are executed.

_____ 12. The president does not need to consult with anyone but his cabinet when he wants a law passed.

_____ 13. The president must sign legislation for it to become law.

_____ 14. Congress passed the National Emergencies Act in 1976 to keep the president's power in check.

_____ 15. If a president does not want a law passed, he throws away the bill when Congress sends it to him.

_____ 16. The president can prevent any bill from becoming law unless Congress passes it over his veto.

_____ 17. The president's cabinet and office can pass laws.

_____ 18. The president always does what his advisors recommend.

Presidency Fill-In

Use the Word Bank at the bottom of the page to fill in the missing words in the paragraphs that follow. All answers will not be used.

As the _____ (1) of the United States, the president helps shape and _____ (2) laws, directs _____ (3) policy, is responsible for national _____ (4), presides at certain ceremonial affairs, and leads his _____(5).

The president does not control the legislative and _____ (6) branches, but can influence lawmaking and does appoint _____ (7) to the Supreme Court. Since no one person can assume all of the presidential duties, assistants are appointed to carry them out. They form the _____ (8) Office. These individuals advise the president on various matters. The _____ (9), consisting of 14 department heads, called secretaries, is also appointed to advise and assist the president. Cabinet members must be approved by _____ (10).

The president is elected to a _____ (11) -year term. No person can be elected to the office of the president more than _____ (12).

Word Bank

legislative	cabinet	judicial
enforce	party	Congress
foreign	House of Representatives	defense
four	six	twice
chief executive	White House	justices
Supreme Court	Capitol	Speaker
once		

The Electoral College

The electoral college was created by the Constitution because the Founding Fathers did not want the president elected by Congress or the people. It is a group of delegates chosen by the voters to elect the president and vice president. On Election Day, the first Tuesday after the first Monday in November, voters mark a ballot for president and vice president. They do not actually vote for the candidates, but they select electors, or delegates, to represent their state in the electoral college. Each state has as many votes in the electoral college as it has senators and representatives. There are 538 electors. The electors meet in December on a date set by law to cast their votes. The results are sent to the president of the Senate who opens them. A candidate must receive 270 or a majority of the electoral votes to win. After two representatives from each body of Congress have counted the electoral votes, the results are officially announced in January. The public knows the results right after the November election because the news media figures them out. These results are not official until the electoral votes have been counted by Congress. A candidate may win the popular vote but lose the election.

Answer true or false to the following statements. The letters in parentheses in the true answers spell out the names of the two presidents who lost the popular vote but won the election.

_____ 1. The electo(r)al res(u)l(t)s are announced in January.

_____ 2. The Founding Fat(h)ers did not want Congr(e)ss to select the p(r)esident.

_____ 3. Each state (h)as the same numb(e)r of electors.

_____ 4. The (f)irst Tuesday after the first M(o)nday in Novembe(r) is Election (D)ay.

_____ 5. Decem(b)er is w(h)en the elector(a)l college meets.

_____ 6. Voters actuall(y) vote for the d(e)legate(s).

_____ 7. Congress (a)nd the public (n)ominate the cand(i)date(s).

_____ 8. A (b)allot is mark(e)d by voters in (N)ovember.

_____ 9. A ma(j)ority of elector(a)l votes (m)akes a w(i)n(n)er.

_____10. T(h)ere (a)re five hund(r)ed thi(r)ty-e(i)ght elector(s).

_____11. The electi(o)n for preside(n)t is t(h)e first Tu(e)sday in Decembe(r).

_____12. It takes 270 elect(o)ral votes to wi(n) the presidency.

The two presidents are _____ and _____.

All About the House

A democratic government needs a legislative body that represents the people. One of the two law-making bodies established as a result of the Great Compromise at the Constitutional Convention was the House of Representatives. The House, as it is often called, is the larger of the two chambers of Congress. Use classroom and library resources to correctly match the items from Lists One and Two. Write the letter from List Two that corresponds to the correct identification on the blank provided.

List One

____ 1. another name for House of Representatives

____ 2. term of service is ____ years

____ 3. total number of representatives allowed

____ 4. leader of House

____ 5. The number of representatives per state is based on _____.

____ 6. _____ has more representatives than any other state.

____ 7. every state has at least this many representatives

____ 8. minimum age to be eligible for election to House

____ 9. Every ten years, a _____ is conducted, which may result in the reapportionment of a state's number of representatives.

____ 10. Of the two bodies of Congress, only the House of Representatives can introduce bills that deal with _____.

List Two

A. population

B. two

C. one

D. four

E. lower house

F. General Assembly

G. census

H. 435

I. 268

J. speaker

K. Whip

L. Texas

M. California

N. taxes

O. treaties

P. 25

Q. 30

Name _____

Senate Facts

Use your research skills to track down the facts that are missing from the passage below. You can use any source you can find to complete the passage.

Compared to the House, the other law-making body of Congress, the Senate is much

_____ (1). The Senate is composed of _____ (2) members

from each _____(3). Therefore, the total number of senators is _____ (4).

Another name for the Senate is the _____ (5). The Senate can

introduce all kinds of legislation except _____ (6) bills. Only the Senate can

approve or reject _____ (7) and certain presidential

_____(8) for government positions, such as judges for federal courts.

Originally the Constitution gave each state _____ (9) the power to select

the senators from each state, but that was changed in 1913 by the _____ (10)

Amendment, which gave the _____ (11) the right to elect them. A senator

serves a _____ (12) -year term. No two senators are elected at the same time

from one _____ (13).

The only duty given the vice president in the _____ (14) is that of

_____ (15) of the Senate. The vice president presides over sessions of the

Senate, but may vote only in the case of a _____ (16). The senators choose a

_____ (17) from their membership to preside over the sessions when

the vice president cannot be there.

Comparing Houses of Congress

Use classroom and library resources to compare and contrast the structure and functions of the Senate and House of Representatives. Write the information in the chart below.

	Senate	House of Representatives
Number of members		
How elected		
Title of members		
Constituents represented		
Qualifications: age, citizenship, & residence		
Length of term		
Title of presiding officer		
Name of current presiding officer		
Impeachment power		
Unique responsibilities		

Making Laws

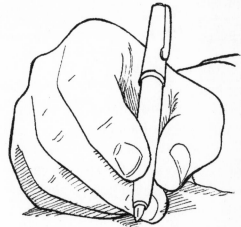

Both senators and representatives may introduce bills, but only members of the House may introduce bills that deal with taxes or spending. Both houses of Congress must pass identical versions of a bill before it can become law. Once a bill is introduced in either house, it goes through almost the same process. After a bill has been approved by Congress, it is sent to the president who may do one of several things. The different steps, from 1 through 9, that make up the process are listed in random order below. Use resource books to help you arrange the steps in correct order from first to last. Write a 1 on the blank in front of the first step, 2 on the blank in front of the second step, etc., through step 9.

_____ A. President signs bill (or, alternatively, does not act on bill within ten-day period after receiving it) and it becomes law, or president vetoes bill (or, alternatively, does not act on bill within ten-day period after receiving it, but Congress adjourns before ten-day period is up), and it is returned to the House.

_____ B. Both houses agree on the bill, and it is signed by the speaker and vice president.

_____ C. Committee releases the bill for the entire House's consideration.

_____ D. Bill is passed by either house.

_____ E. Bill is introduced and assigned to a committee.

_____ F. Bill is sent to the other house for input and consideration.

_____ G. Congress makes changes in bill to satisfy president's wishes, and it is returned to president who then signs it, or two thirds of both houses vote for it as it is and the bill becomes a law despite the president's veto.

_____ H. Differences between two houses are worked out by a joint conference committee.

_____ I. Bill is sent to president for his/her signature.

Impeachment

The Constitution states that the president, vice president, and all civil officers of the United States may "be removed from office on impeachment for, and conviction of, treason, bribery, or other high crimes and misdemeanors." The House of Representatives has the sole power to impeach or bring charges against government officials (except for members of Congress). A majority vote of members of the House is needed to impeach. The Senate has the sole power to try or judge the impeachment case. A two-thirds vote of the senators present is needed for conviction. If an official is found guilty, the official can be removed from office. When a president is tried, the chief justice of the Supreme Court presides over the Senate. In other cases the vice president presides. One president, Richard Nixon, resigned the presidency in 1974 rather than face certain impeachment. Two presidents have been impeached by the House. In both cases, the Senate failed to get the two-thirds vote necessary for conviction. President Bill Clinton was impeached in 1998. The other president was impeached in 1868. The last name of that president will appear in the boxes after you fill in the answers to the questions below.

1. Who presides over the trial of the president?
   _ _ _ _ _ □ _ _ _ _ _ _

2. Who brings impeachment charges?
   _ □ _ . _ _

3. What vote is needed for conviction?
   _ _ _ _-_ □ _ _ _ _

4. The House may not impeach members of ___.
   _ _ □ _ _ _ _

5. Who tries the impeachment cases?
   □ _ _ _ _ _

6. How many presidents have been tried?
   _ _ □

7. How many presidential convictions have there been?
   □ _ _ _

The president's name is Andrew _____.

The Judicial Branch

The Supreme Court heads the judicial branch of the United States government. It is the only court established by the Constitution.

The Supreme Court usually makes decisions of national importance. The court acts within the laws stated by the Constitution. Because the wording of the Constitution is sometimes hard to understand, it can be difficult to interpret the law. That is one of the duties of the Supreme Court. When the court does make a decision, all other courts in the country must follow that decision to guarantee equal legal justice to all Americans. The Constitution also gives the Supreme Court the power to judge whether federal, state, and local governments are acting within the law and also to decide if an action of the president is constitutional.

Answer the questions below. The letters in boxes in the answers when unscrambled will spell out what a judge in the Supreme Court is called.

1. The Supreme Court usually only hears what kind of cases?

　_　_　□　_　_　_　_　_

2. What set of laws guides the Supreme Court's decisions?

　_　_　_　_　_　□　_　_　□　_　_　_

3. The Supreme Court heads what branch of government?

　□　_　_　_　_　□　_　_

4. What other courts are there in the United States that must follow the decisions of the Supreme Court?

　_　_　_　□　_　_　_

　_　_　_　_　_　_　□　_　_

5. What is a judge that sits on the Supreme Court bench called?

　_　_　_　_　_　_　_　_

The Supreme Court

The Supreme Court is the only court created by the Constitution. Nine justices sit on the Supreme Court, including the chief justice. The justices are appointed by the president for life. It is their job to hear the most important and often the most controversial cases in the land. It can hear cases involving disputes between states or when a foreign country is involved. Most of the cases are appeals or requests to review lower court rulings. Each year, thousands of petitions (requests to hear appeals) are sent to the Supreme Court. Only a few of these are actually heard by the court. At least four justices must agree before a petition can be heard. After a case is argued before the court, the justices vote on it. At least five votes one way or another are required to reach a decision. Once a decision is reached, the ruling is written up. Past rulings are used to guide future decisions in similar cases. Since the Supreme Court is the court of last appeal, its decisions are final and must be followed by all other courts.

Below are descriptions of two actual Supreme Court cases. If you had been one of the justices, how would you have voted?

1. Mr. Gideon, who was arrested for petty larceny, asked the court to appoint a lawyer to represent him. His request was turned down, and Gideon represented himself. He lost the case and was sentenced to prison. While in prison, he petitioned the Supreme Court to hear his case, arguing that since he did not have a court-appointed lawyer, he did not have a fair trial. What do you think?

   _____

   _____

2. Mr. Wong was born in California to parents who were both citizens of China. When he returned from a brief visit to China, U.S. Government immigration officials refused to readmit him to this country. They claimed he was not an American citizen because the Fourteenth Amendment did not apply in his case. What do you think?

   _____

   _____

Important Supreme Court Decisions

Some important Supreme Court cases are described on the left below. The names of the cases are listed on the right. Match the case with its name by writing the correct letter on the blank in front of the number.

Cases

_____ 1. The court established the power to review acts of Congress and declare laws unconstitutional if they violate the Constitution.

_____ 2. The court declared the Missouri Compromise of 1820 unconstitutional.

_____ 3. The court ruled that the Bill of Rights applied to the states.

_____ 4. The court ruled that separate schools for blacks and whites were inherently unequal.

_____ 5. The court ruled that a woman's decision to have an abortion should be left to her and to her physician.

_____ 6. The court ruled that the president did not have temporary immunity from lawsuit for actions not related to official duties.

_____ 7. The court ruled that suspects of a crime must be informed of their rights.

_____ 8. The court ruled that separate but equal facilities for blacks and whites on trains did not violate civil rights of blacks.

_____ 9. The court ruled that neither the states nor Congress could limit the terms of members of Congress.

_____10. The court ruled that school officials could not require a pupil to recite a state-composed prayer.

Name

A. *Miranda v. Arizona*, 1966

B. *Brown v. Board of Education*, 1954

C. *Clinton v. Jones*, 1997

D. *Roe v. Wade*, 1973

E. *Marbury v. Madison*, 1803

F. *Gitlow v. New York*, 1925

G. *U.S. Term Limits Inc. v. Thorton*, 1995

H. *Engel v. Vitale*, 1962

I. *Dred Scott v. Sanford*, 1857

J. *Plessy v. Ferguson*, 1896

Political Dictionary

How is your political vocabulary? Below on the right is a list of vocabulary words that every politically savvy person ought to know. The column on the left lists the definitions for those words. Your task is to use classroom or library reference books to match the words and definitions correctly.

____ 1. a statement of government policy

____ 2. to impose or collect money required by the government, such as an income tax

____ 3. an independent politician; in 1884, one who left the Republican Party

____ 4. a group of electors that elects the president and vice president of the United States

____ 5. related and limited to one's own country

____ 6. dividing district boundaries to give one party the political advantage

____ 7. government official skilled in negotiation

____ 8. executive power to stop a legislative measure

____ 9. to get more votes than the other candidates, but less than a majority (50% or more) of the votes

____ 10. officer in charge of legislative body

____ 11. unofficial, but often influential, advisors

____ 12. a member of the electoral college

____ 13. closed meeting of political party

____ 14. helps organize and unify his/her party's legislators

____ 15. a little known contestant for political office

____ 16. appointments made in exchange for political favors

____ 17. a representative at a party convention

A. electoral college
B. plurality
C. whip
D. domestic
E. gerrymandering
F. levy
G. caucus
H. Speaker
I. elector
J. Kitchen Cabinet
K. dark horse
L. veto
M. diplomat
N. spoils system
O. mugwump
P. delegate
Q. doctrine

The Meaning of Democracy

The American system of government is based upon the concept of *democracy*. What does this word mean to you? Inside the box on the left below, write down your own ideas about democracy and examples of democracy. Then, find definitions and examples of democracy in classroom and library resource books and write them down inside the box on the right. Compare the two lists. How are they similar and different?

My Own Ideas and Examples . . .

Definitions and Examples from Books

American Society

A wide variety of ethnic backgrounds, races, religions, classes, and languages shape American society. Some important factors that helped shape American society are listed below. Research each factor. Then write down inside the box a reason why each factor was important.

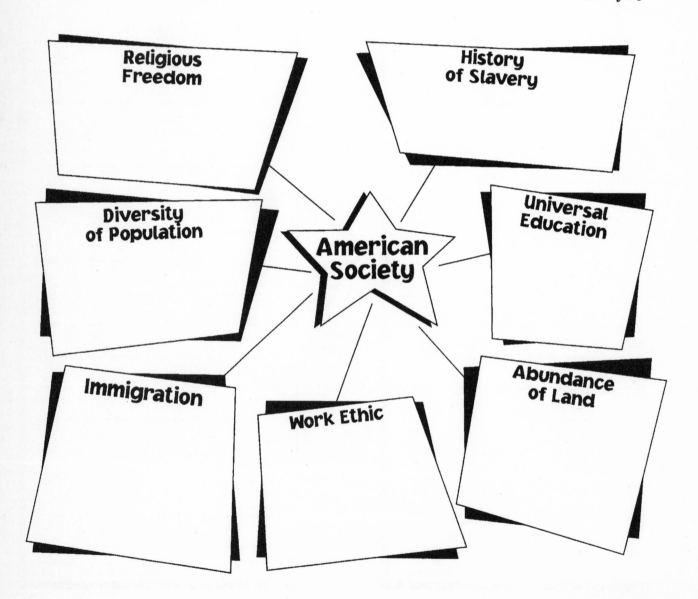

Religious Freedom

History of Slavery

Diversity of Population

Universal Education

American Society

Immigration

Work Ethic

Abundance of Land

IF87050 *U.S. Government*

Values and Government

The values held by a nation and its people influence each new generation of citizens. For example, our nation is based on the ideal that all people are created equal. This powerful value has motivated Americans past and present to fight against racial and gender discrimination. Do you share the same values as your classmates? After you respond to the questions below, trade your paper with another student and compare your answers.

What is one thing you would change . . .

in the world?

_____
_____
_____

in your state?

_____
_____
_____

in your town/city?

_____
_____
_____

in your school?

_____
_____
_____

Expressing Our Ideals

The statement on the left below were taken from some very important documents. The statements express ideals and beliefs about natural rights of men and women everywhere in the world. Study the important documents listed on the right. Then match the document and statement.

Statement

Document

____ 1. ". . . human rights should be protected by the rule of law."

____ 2. "We hold these truths to be self-evident, that all men are created equal."

____ 3. "No freeman shall be taken, or imprisoned, or outlawed, or exiled, or in any way harmed . . . except by the legal judgement of his peers or by the law of the land."

____ 4. "All persons shall be entitled to the full and equal enjoyment of . . . any place of public accommodation . . . without discrimination or segregation . . ."

____ 5. ". . government of the people, by the people, for the people, shall not perish from the earth."

____ 6. "Congress shall make no law . . . abridging [depriving] the freedom of speech . . ."

____ 7. "We the People of the United States, in Order to form a more perfect Union, establish Justice . . . and secure the Blessings of Liberty. . ."

A. Civil Rights Act of 1964

B. First Amendment of U.S. Constitution

C. UN Declaration of Human Rights

D. Abraham Lincoln's "Gettysburg Address"

E. Preamble to the U.S. Constitution

F. Declaration of Independence

G. Magna Carta

Real and Ideal

Ideals are standards of perfection. They are the ultimate aim of an endeavor. For the United States and its citizens, the ultimate aim of public life is to form a more perfect union, or nation, by expanding and enhancing liberty, justice, and the common good. *Reality,* on the other hand, refers to the way things are. The gap, then, between reality and ideals can be called the unfinished business of America. When it comes to America's ideals, how far away do you think the nation is from perfection? For the statements below, indicate your opinion by circling one of the following: strongly agree (SA), agree (A), disagree (D), strongly disagree (SD), or don't know (DK). After you finish, pair up with another student and compare opinions.

1. America is a just society. SA   A   D   SD   DK
2. Some people are treated better than others. SA   A   D   SD   DK
3. America says one thing but does another. SA   A   D   SD   DK
4. Poor people in America have equal access to the judicial system. SA   A   D   SD   DK
5. America is a land of opportunity. SA   A   D   SD   DK
6. People are free to express their views without fear. SA   A   D   SD   DK
7. People are knowledgeable about their government and well-informed on the issues. SA   A   D   SD   DK
8. People care about themselves and not about the common good. SA   A   D   SD   DK
9. People respect the rights of others. SA   A   D   SD   DK
10. America denies liberty and equality to many of its citizens. SA   A   D   SD   DK

A Citizenship Primer

Below are some statements about the meaning and nature of American citizenship. Some of the statements are true and some are false. Can you tell the difference? Use classroom and library resources to check for their accuracy. Then, circle either "true" or "false" in front of each statement. In addition, for each erroneous statement, write the statement so that it is factually correct on the blank provided.

1. True   False   Anyone born in the United States is a U.S. citizen.

   _____

2. True   False   To become a U.S. citizen, an alien must live in the United States for three years.

   _____

3. True   False   An alien does not need to read, write, and speak English to become a U.S. citizen.

   _____

4. True   False   Americans are citizens of both their state and the United States.

   _____

5. True   False   American citizenship confers equal rights under the law.

   _____

Who Represents You?

Few Americans can identify the key people elected to serve them. Who represents you in the legislative and executive branches of your local, state, and national governments? Find out, and write their names under or beside each title.

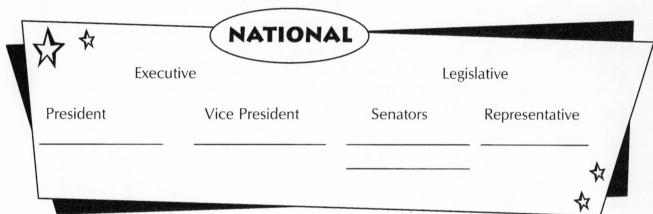

NATIONAL

Executive

President   Vice President

_____   _____

Legislative

Senators   Representative

_____   _____

_____

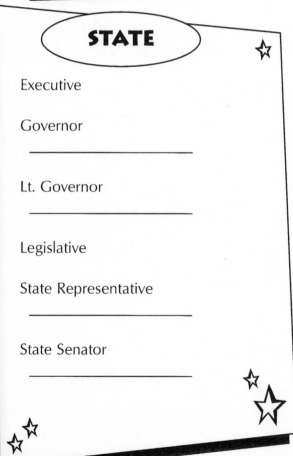

STATE

Executive

Governor

_____

Lt. Governor

_____

Legislative

State Representative

_____

State Senator

_____

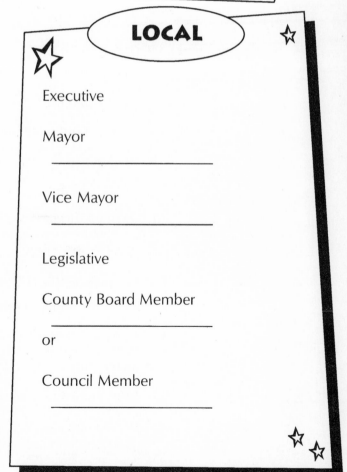

LOCAL

Executive

Mayor

_____

Vice Mayor

_____

Legislative

County Board Member

_____

or

Council Member

_____

Rights and Responsibilities

You have probably heard the expression "Get a life!" An important part of your life, both now and in the future, is your civic life. What is your civic life? *Civics* refers to the political rights and responsibilities of citizenship. The word *civics* comes from the Latin word *civis,* which means citizen. *Political rights* are powers or privileges to which all citizens are due or entitled. *Political responsibilities* refer to obligations and actions regarding the exercise of political rights for the betterment of society. An important political right is the right to vote; a political responsibility directly associated with this right is deciding whether and how to vote. Which statements below are rights, and which ones are responsibilities? Write the word "right" or "responsibility" on the blank in front of each of the statements below.

_____ 1. to a fair trial in a court of law

_____ 2. to a free press

_____ 3. to vote

_____ 4. to respect the rights of others

_____ 5. to speak freely

_____ 6. to assemble

_____ 7. to criticize the government

_____ 8. to travel between states

_____ 9. to exercise the right to vote

_____ 10. to take an active part in civic affairs

_____ 11. to obey the laws

_____ 12. to serve on juries

_____ 13. to serve in the armed forces

_____ 14. to be protected from hate speech

_____ 15. to write a letter to the editor

_____ 16. to pay taxes

_____ 17. to petition the government

Democratic Quiz

Below are some traits that are important to the preservation and improvement of American democracy. Circle the score that best describes students at your school.

3 = very true for your school
2 = somewhat true for your school
1 = not at all true for your school

At my school, most students demonstrate the following traits most of the time:

1. Individual responsibility (e.g., fulfilling one's responsibilities)	3	2	1
2. Self-discipline (e.g., obeying reasonable rules)	3	2	1
3. Civility (e.g., treating other people with respect)	3	2	1
4. Honesty (e.g., telling the truth)	3	2	1
5. Respect for the law (e.g., abiding by rules)	3	2	1
6. Open-mindedness (e.g., considering the viewpoint of others)	3	2	1
7. Negotiation and Compromise (e.g., trying to reach agreements with others)	3	2	1
8. Persistence (e.g., staying with the task or goal and not giving up)	3	2	1
9. Civic-mindedness (e.g., showing concern for one's community and nation)	3	2	1
10. Compassion (e.g., concern for the well-being of others)	3	2	1
11. Patriotism (e.g., loyalty to the values and principles underlying the American constitutional democracy)	3	2	1

Protecting Your Rights

Due process refers to the right of every citizen to be protected from unlawful and/or abusive actions by government. The major due process protections are listed on the right. A definition of each protection is listed on the left. Use classroom and library resources to correctly match them.

Definition

Protection

_____ 1. Every person accused of a crime must be represented by an attorney.

A. habeas corpus

_____ 2. A group of individuals are chosen to make a decision about the guilt or innocence of an accused person.

B. presumption of innocence

C. fair notice

_____ 3. A court of justice must be comprised of objective and fair-minded officials.

D. impartial tribunal

_____ 4. This principle ensures that a person found not guilty cannot be tried again on the same charges.

E. speedy and public trials

F. right to counsel

_____ 5 An accused person has a right to be informed of the charges against him/her.

G. trial by jury

_____ 6. A person accused of a crime is still considered to be free from guilt until proven otherwise in a court of law.

H. right against self-incrimination

_____ 7. An accused person does not have to give evidence which could be used against him or her.

I. protection against double jeopardy

J. right of appeal

_____ 8. A person found guilty of a crime can ask a higher court to rehear his or her case.

_____ 9. A person accused of a crime has the right to be brought to trial as quickly as possible in a court room that is open to the public.

_____ 10. This court order demands that the person in custody be brought to court and shown the reasons for detention.

Wrongs and Rights

On the left below are examples of rights that have been violated, or wrongs. On the right below, are the rights themselves, as they are stated in the Constitution. Match what happened (the wrong) with the right that was violated (right).

Wrongs

____ 1. A person is told he cannot criticize the president.

____ 2. A state forbids an 18-year-old citizen from registering to vote.

____ 3. A person is fined $25,000 for loitering.

____ 4. Torture is used to force a confession.

____ 5. All children in a public school are told to say aloud a prayer.

____ 6. A person is kept in jail for 18 months before trial.

____ 7. A person is told he cannot ride on a public bus because he is black.

____ 8. A person's house is broken into by police without a search warrant.

____ 9. A state is told it cannot keep a militia or home guard.

____ 10. A person is forced to provide shelter to soldiers during peacetime.

Rights

A. The right of a person to be secure in their . . . house . . . against unreasonable searches . . . shall not be violated.

B. Excessive fines [shall not be] imposed.

C. Congress shall make no law . . . abridging freedom of speech.

D. No person shall be compelled . . . to be a witness against himself.

E. No state shall . . . deny any person . . . the equal protection of the law.

F. No citizen 18 years of age or older can have the right to vote taken away because of age.

G. The right of the people to keep and bear arms shall not be infringed.

H. Congress shall make no law respecting an establishment of religion.

I. The accused shall have the right to a speedy and public trial.

J. No soldier shall, in time of peace, be quartered in any house, without the consent of the owner.

Civil Disobedience

Throughout history, Americans have used civil disobedience as a means of social protest. *Civil disobedience* is the nonviolent confrontation of injustice by refusing to obey any law that is believed to be unjust. Four important Americans who used civil disobedience to promote individual rights and the common good are named below. Use classroom and library resources to learn about their beliefs and actions. Then, briefly describe how each used civil disobedience during his or her time in history.

Henry David Thoreau

_____
_____
_____

Susan B. Anthony

_____
_____
_____

Martin Luther King, Jr.

_____
_____
_____

Cesar Chavez

_____
_____
_____

Domestic Policies

Name _____

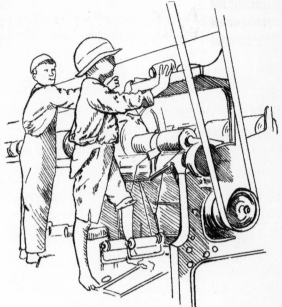

The national government has many major responsibilities for domestic policies. *Domestic* refers to policies related and limited to one's own country. These policies have significant consequences for all Americans. On the left side of the chart below is a list of important domestic policies. Examples of both historical and current policies are included. Your task is to investigate each policy using resources from the classroom and library. Then explain how and why each of these policies affects the daily lives of Americans, both past and present.

Policy	**Effects of Policy**
1. Pure Food and Drug Act	_____
2. Environmental Protection Act	_____
3. civil rights laws	_____
4. child labor laws	_____
5. minimum wage laws	_____
6. Social Security	_____
7. Medicare	_____

Foreign Policy

Below are listed some historical and contemporary examples of important U.S. government foreign policies. Use classroom and library resources to learn about them. Then briefly describe the significant consequences of each policy on the daily lives of people.

Foreign Policy   **Consequences**

1. Monroe Doctrine _____
   _____

2. Marshall Plan _____
   _____

3. Truman Doctrine _____
   _____

4. immigration acts _____
   _____

5. foreign aid_____
   _____

6. arms control _____
   _____

7. human rights_____
   _____

Comparative Governments

Facts about some major foreign governments are presented on the left. A list of nations is on the right. Match the nation with the appropriate information by writing the correct letter on the blank in front of the number.

Facts

_____ 1. has 650 members in the House of Commons

_____ 2. The legislative branch is called the *Riksdag*.

_____ 3. has a president and a parliament elected by people

_____ 4. The Communist Party rules the country.

_____ 5. Parliament consists of a single-chamber House of Representatives.

_____ 6. The government's legal system is based on the teachings of Islam.

_____ 7. The parliament is called the Knesset.

_____ 8. Nelson Mandela was the first black person to be elected president.

_____ 9. The parliament is called the National Diet.

_____ 10. The seat of government is Moscow.

_____ 11. Parliament consists of the House of Commons and Senate.

_____ 12. It is called the most democratic nation in Central America.

Nations

A. Costa Rica
B. Japan
C. Russia
D. New Zealand
E. Britain
F. France
G. South Africa
H. China
I. Sweden
J. Saudi Arabia
K. Canada
L. Israel

Write a brief description of one of the governments above.

_____

_____

_____

Dictatorships and Democracies

After you read the following information about dictatorships and democracies, fill in the comparison chart below. A *dictatorship* is a nation whose government is completely under the control of a dictator, or all-powerful ruler. The twentieth century saw the rise of many dictatorships. Near the end of World War I, Russia became a Communist dictatorship. In 1933 Adolf Hitler set up a dictatorship in Germany. Dictatorships were also set up in Italy, Spain, and most of the Balkan nations.
Although dictatorships may have written constitutions and elections, the constitutions do not give freedom to their people, and the elections are controlled by the government. In a dictatorship, people are not allowed to disagree with the government. The idea of individual rights is not valued in a dictatorship. Instead, individuals are valued only to the extent they can serve the government. Democracies are the opposite of dictatorships. Democratic government is considered to be the servant of the people, rather than the other way around. Democracies are based on the idea that the people rule. Authority to govern comes from the people. In a democracy, fair and free elections are held regularly. Without an informed and questioning citizenry, a democracy could not survive.

COMPARING DICTATORSHIPS AND DEMOCRACIES

CHARACTERISTICS OF GOVERNMENT	DICTATORSHIPS	DEMOCRACIES
CONDITION OF THE PEOPLE		
POLITICAL PROCESS		
DICTATORSHIPS		
DEMOCRACIES		
STATUS OF INDIVIDUAL		

International Organizations

Some of the major international organizations are listed below. Use classroom and library resources to learn about the purpose and function of each one. Then write your descriptions on the blanks provided.

1. United Nations (UN)

   _____

   _____

   _____

2. International Red Cross

   _____

   _____

   _____

3. North Atlantic Treaty Organization (NATO)

   _____

   _____

   _____

4. World Council of Churches

   _____

   _____

   _____

5. Organization of American States (OAS)

   _____

   _____

   _____

6. Amnesty International

   _____

   _____

   _____

7. World Court

   _____

   _____

   _____

Name _____

The United States and the World

Because the United States is part of an interconnected world, Americans are affected by other nations and other nations are influenced by American policies and society. Six of the most important ways that nations interact with one another are listed below. Search through newspapers and magazines for international news stories related to each of the types of interaction listed below. Then, after you have read the stories, use the information to fill in facts related to the United States and another nation of your choice for each means of interaction.

Types of Interaction	United States	_____ (Write name of nation)
Trade		
Diplomacy		
Treaties and agreements		
Humanitarian aid		
Economic incentives and sanctions		
Military force and the threat of force		

Name _____

Government in Your Life

To examine the influence government has on you, answer the questions below. After you complete the questionnaire, pair up with another student and compare your answers.

1. Who is your favorite or most admired leader in American government, past or present?

   _____

2. What do you most admire about the person you named above?

   _____

3. What law or rule—at the school, community, state, or national level—do you think is most beneficial?

   _____

4. How does the rule or law identified above benefit you and society?

   _____

5. What law or rule at the school, community, state, or national level do you think is not beneficial, or even harmful?

   _____

6. How does the rule or law identified above not benefit, or harm, you and society?

   _____

7. If you had the power to enact a new rule or law, what would it be? Why?

   _____

8. How important is government in your life (circle one)?

   Very Important   Somewhat Important   Not Important

Community Needs

Imagine you have been elected to city council. As a city council board member, it is your responsibility to fight for the needs of your district. Below is a list of proposals for meeting those needs. Although it would be nice to do everything on the list, the city can afford to only do a few of them. The city has a total of $1 million to spend. Your task is to identify proposals that you personally believe are most important to fund by ranking them from 1 for the most important to 12 for the least important. The cost for each proposal is in parentheses. Remember you cannot spent more than $1 million, so consider the different needs carefully. After you rank the proposals, discuss your rankings with another student.

____ buy land for a new park ($500,000)

____ build a new parking lot ($300,000)

____ add ten members to the police force ($200,000)

____ provide day-care services for the needy ($100,000)

____ fund a baseball park ($700,000)

____ build another elementary school ($800,000)

____ add a wing to the hospital ($400,000)

____ build low-income housing ($1,000,000)

____ develop a mass transit bus system ($400,000)

____ expand the library ($500,000)

____ buy a new fire truck ($300,000)

____ build a produce/fruit/vegetable market ($100,000)

Make a Statement!

Identify a public goal for which you have concern, such as increasing the safety of the community, improving local transportation facilities, or providing opportunities for education and recreation. Then, use the space below to make a colorful poster that expresses your views and communicates them forcefully.

Civics and Group Membership

Clubs, teams, bands, squads, classes, families—chances are, you belong to many different groups. With membership in each of these groups comes different rights and responsibilities. In the space provided below, list two groups to which you belong. Then, for each group, list three rights you have as a group member and three responsibilities you have as a group member.

Group:

Rights:

1. _____

2. _____

3. _____

Responsibilities:

1. _____

2. _____

3. _____

Group:

Rights:

1. _____

2. _____

3. _____

Responsibilities:

1. _____

2. _____

3. _____

Putting Civic Ideal into Practice

There are many associations and groups that provide opportunities for citizens to participate in the political process. Use classroom and library resources to find out about the prominent associations and groups listed below. Then, briefly describe the role each one plays in local, state, or national politics.

1. AFL-CIO _____

   _____

2. National Education Association _____

   _____

3. Chamber of Commerce _____

   _____

4. Common Cause _____

   _____

5. League of Women Voters _____

   _____

6. American Medical Association _____

   _____

7. National Rifle Association _____

   _____

8. Greenpeace _____

   _____

9. National Association for the Advancement of Colored People (NAACP) _____

   _____

10. World Wildlife Federation _____

   _____

Participating in Government

An *agenda* is a list of things that need to be done. *The public agenda* refers to numerous opportunities within the American political system for individual choice and participation. Below is a chart showing some problems or issues that need public attention and some opportunities for participation. Put check marks inside the boxes to show issues and opportunities for dealing with them that particularly interest you.

Opportunities for Participation	Issues						
	Crime	Health Care	Education	Child Care	Environment	Drug Abuse	(Write issue of your choice.)
Join interest groups.							
Make presentations.							
Write letters to public officials and newspapers.							
Interview government officials.							
Visit local governmental agencies.							
Participate in community service activities.							
Make posters and display them in prominent places.							

The Changing Role of Women

In a democracy, all of the people are free to participate in government. Ideally, that means being knowledgeable about world, national, state, and local issues. One issue deals with the changing role of women in society. For centuries, women were expected to stay close to home, do household chores, and raise a family. Married women back then were called "homemakers" and "housewives." Since the 1960s the role of women has changed dramatically. Today women increasingly pursue opportunities in education, business, government, and the military—opportunities that were once open only to men. Now, the tendency is for both husband and wife to work outside the home, and traditional duties regarding child rearing and housekeeping have shifted between couples, or have been redistributed to others. What is your own opinion about these changes? Write your thoughts below. Then, trade papers with another student and compare your opinions.

My thoughts on the changing role of women . . .

_____
_____
_____
_____
_____
_____
_____
_____
_____
_____
_____
_____

Decision-Making: Where Do You Stand?

Most big problems in need of solutions are difficult and complex. Take smoking, for example. There is ample evidence that smoking causes cancer, heart disease, emphysema, chronic bronchitis, miscarriages, and infant deaths. In addition, tobacco smoke in the workplace and social settings is believed to raise the risk of lung cancer for nonsmokers. The answer to the smoking problem seems clear and simple: Smoking should be completely banned. But wait a minute! Haven't people been growing and smoking tobacco for centuries? What about all of the people whose livelihood depends on the tobacco industry? If smoking were banned, thousands of tobacco farmers would be out of work. So would the employees of companies that make cigarettes and cigars. If smoking were illegal, would smokers just seek out illegal cigarettes? Do we really want to create a new category of criminals: the sellers of illegal cigarettes and the smokers who purchase them?

In the space provided below, present two stands on the smoking issue. First, use classroom and library sources to investigate the issue thoroughly. Then, write a sentence that argues for a complete ban on smoking followed by another sentence that argues against a complete ban. If you wish to write more, you may continue on the back of this page. Finally, circle "yes," "no," or "don't know" to indicate your own stand on the issue. After you have finished, exchange papers with another student and read each other's sentences. Do you agree or disagree on the issue?

1. Smoking should be completely banned because . . .

   _____

   _____

2. Smoking should not be completely banned because . . .

   _____

   _____

3. Based on your study of the issue,
   should smoking be completely banned?   YES   NO   DON'T KNOW

Evaluating Political Messages

How influential are the media on American political life? The chart below lists some major opportunities the media provide for individuals to communicate their concerns and positions on current issues. Search for examples of each of them on TV and radio, on the Internet (under teacher and/or parental supervision), and in current newspapers, news magazines, and other print sources. Then for each one, identify the concern and position inside the boxes on the chart.

Media & Format	Concern	Position
Letter to the Editor		
TV Talk Show		
Radio Talk Show		
Opinion/Editorial Page		
Public Opinion Poll		
Newsletter		
Internet		

Citizen Checklist

Below is a list of questions. A good citizen needs to know the answers to these questions. How many do you know? Write the answers on the line under each question. If you do not know an answer, ask your parents or another adult to help you.

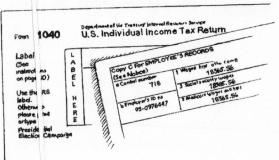

☐ How do you apply for a Social Security card?

_____

☐ How do you get legal advice?

_____

☐ How, and to whom, do you report a crime?

_____

☐ How do you sign up to vote?

_____

☐ How do you find your polling place?

_____

☐ How do you file a tax return?

_____

☐ How do you find out what the minimum wage is?

_____

☐ Where do you go, and what do you need to know, to get a driver's license?

_____

Becoming a Citizen

After you read the following passage, take the citizenship quiz.

There are two ways to become an American citizen. People born in the United States are *native-born* citizens. People born outside the United States can become native-born citizens if at least one of their parents is a citizen who has resided in the United States. Immigrants, or people who come here to live from other countries, can become *naturalized* citizens.

The following conditions must be met for most people to become naturalized citizens: be at least 18 years old, live in the United States five years, demonstrate knowledge of the English language, be of good moral character, demonstrate knowledge of American history and government, and take an oath of allegiance to the United States and its laws.

Citizenship Quiz

1. Are you a citizen of the United States? _____

2. Can a person born outside the United States become a native-born citizen? _____

3. If a person is not born in the United States, how can he/she become an American citizen?

   _____

   _____

   _____

4. Should someone who wants to become a naturalized citizen be required to demonstrate understanding of English and of American history and government? Give reasons for your answer.

   _____

   _____

   _____

5. Find a copy of the Oath of Allegiance in an encyclopedia and read it. Would you take the oath? Explain your answer below.

   _____

   _____

   _____

Resolving Conflicts

Good citizens know how to help others resolve conflicts constructively. Below are some situations that contain conflicts. For each one, explain what you would do to resolve the conflict peacefully.

1. A smaller kid is victimized by a bigger kid.

   _____

2. Two kids are arguing about who sits where at lunch.

   _____

   _____

   _____

   _____

   _____

3. A younger brother is upset because his older sister gets a bigger weekly allowance.

   _____

   _____

   _____

   _____

   _____

Asking the Right Questions

To make wise decisions, you must ask the right questions. For example, if you are trying to decide which shirt to buy, you would probably ask yourself questions like "How much do the shirts cost?" and "Which shirt do I like the best?" Good citizens also must ask the right questions about local, state, and national issues. List four questions that you would want to ask for each of the issues described below.

Issue #1—The city board is debating about whether or not to create a nature center.
Questions:

1. _____
2. _____
3. _____
4. _____

Issue # 2—Members of a Rifle and Hunters' Club want to use the school's auditorium for a Saturday meeting and firearms exhibit.
Questions:

1. _____
2. _____
3. _____
4. _____

Issue #3—The school board debates changing from a 9-month to a 12-month school year.
Questions:

1. _____
2. _____
3. _____
4. _____

Community Resources

A good citizen is aware of the resources available in his/her community. The telephone book can tell you a lot about the resources available in your community. Use a local telephone book to find the services listed below. Name the organization/service and local phone number on the lines provided. To find the information quickly, use the index found in the Yellow Pages and the Blue Pages of government listings.

Drug abuse and addiction information and treatment

_____

_____

Social service organizations

_____

_____

Health department

_____

_____

Human services

_____

_____

Parks and recreation

_____

_____

Voter registration

_____

_____

Minority programs and affirmative action

_____

_____

Economic development

_____

_____

Economic Decision-Making

Every day, you buy and use products and services. As a consumer of goods and services, you need to be aware of how the government helps the consumer make good economic choices. The government requires manufacturers to list ingredient and nutrient information on food container labels. Use the label from a container of food to answer the questions. Note: Ingredients are listed on the label in order of their quantity, i.e., there is more of the first ingredient listed than the second ingredient listed, etc.

1. What does the "U.S. government" mark on the container mean? _____

2. What is the serving size? _____

3. How many servings are there per container? _____

4. How many calories are there per serving? _____

5. What ingredient does the food contain more of than any other? _____

6. How many grams does one serving contain of the following:
   Protein?_____
   Carbohydrate?_____
   Fat?_____

7. What is the percentage of U.S. RDA (recommended daily allowance) per serving of the following:
   Protein?_____
   Iron?_____
   Vitamin A?_____
   Vitamin C?_____
   Niacin?_____
   Riboflavin?_____

Family Decisions

According to government statistics, an average family's greatest expense is for housing, followed by food, and then transportation. Ask members of your family to tell you about family expenses. Then, using numbers 1 to 7, list the following items in order of expense to your family. Place 1 next to the item of greatest expense, 2 next to the item that ranks next highest, and so on. At the bottom of the page, list some items on which you personally spend the most money.

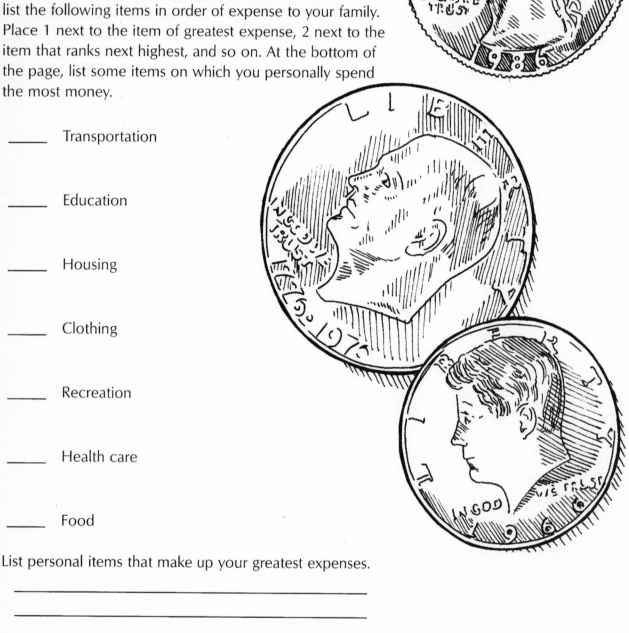

_____ Transportation

_____ Education

_____ Housing

_____ Clothing

_____ Recreation

_____ Health care

_____ Food

List personal items that make up your greatest expenses.

_____

_____

_____

_____

Eye Witness Account

Use information from encyclopedias and other sources to explain why you would have liked to witness the following important political events from history.

1. Thomas Jefferson writing the Declaration of Independence

   _____
   _____
   _____

2. the debate at the Constitutional Convention of 1787

   _____
   _____
   _____

3. the moment the Bill of Rights was ratified

   _____
   _____
   _____

4. the moment the Emancipation Proclamation took effect in the South

   _____
   _____
   _____

5. the day the U.S. Supreme Court made its decision in the *Brown v. Board of Education* case

   _____
   _____
   _____

If You Could Vote Tomorrow

If you could vote tomorrow, what three domestic issues would you want to vote on? Use the space below to write your answer, and be as specific as possible.

Issue #1

_____

_____

_____

_____

_____

_____

Issue #2

_____

_____

_____

_____

_____

_____

Issue #3

_____

_____

_____

_____

_____

Activities for President Cards and Time Line

This section suggests ideas for using the president cards and presidential time line that begin on page 84.

To prepare the president cards, do the following: (1) photocopy the president cards and presidential time line pages (you will need one copy per set; to allow multiple teams to use a complete set of cards, make multiple copies); (2) cut out the cards (portrait for the front, information for the back); (3) align the frontside and backside of each card so that the portrait and information are showing; (4) use glue or paste (just a tiny amount along the edges) to attach the front of the card (portrait) to the back of the card (information); and (5) laminate each card.

To prepare the time line, trim it neatly and laminate it.

Students can use the president cards and presidential time line in the following ways:
• As an aid to the study of information about the presidents
• As a tool for practicing chronological, classification, and comparing skills
• As a basis for individual, team, and classroom games

Using the President Cards and Presidential Time Line
PRESIDENTIAL CLASSIFICATION
Type of activity: In this game players try to identify as many presidents as they can that fit the classification. For example, if the classification is *Republican,* then players would name presidents that were (are) members of the Republican Party.

Directions for independent play: Write the classifications on the board or at a learning center. Individual players play the game independently throughout the school day. Given a limited time period, the player compiles a list of presidents that fit each classification, using the president cards. At the end of the time period, each player turns in his/her lists, which are checked for accuracy. The player with the most complete correct lists wins.

Directions for team play: Divide the class into two or more teams, each with a captain. Provide each team with a set of president cards and let the captain deal out the cards to members of his/her team. Read aloud the following directions: This is a game in which we try to find as many presidents that fit each of the classifications. As players use the president cards to classify the presidents, the captain records answers and lists his/her own contributions as well. At the end of a limited time period, each captain will read the list compiled by his/her team. Teams score a point for each correct classification.

Classification	Presidents
President in Twentieth century	McKinley, T. Roosevelt, Taft, Wilson, Harding, Coolidge, Hoover, F. D. Roosevelt, Truman, Eisenhower, Kennedy, L. B. Johnson, Nixon, Ford, Carter, Reagan, Bush, Clinton
Member of Whig Party	W. H. Harrison, Tyler, Taylor, Fillmore
Died in office	W. H. Harrison, Taylor, Lincoln, Garfield, McKinley, Harding, F. D. Roosevelt, Kennedy
Elected to two (or more) terms	Washington, Jefferson, Madison, Monroe, Jackson, Lincoln, Grant, Cleveland, Wilson, F. D. Roosevelt, Eisenhower, Nixon, Reagan, Clinton
First name is William	W. H. Harrison, McKinley, Taft, Clinton
First name is James	Madison, Monroe, Polk, Buchanan, Garfield, Carter
Served as vice president	J. Adams, Jefferson, Van Buren, Tyler, Fillmore, A. Johnson, Arthur, Coolidge, Truman, Nixon, L. B. Johnson, Ford, Bush
Born in Virginia	Washington, Jefferson, Madison, Monroe, W. H. Harrison, Tyler, Taylor, Wilson
Born west of Mississippi River	Hoover, Truman, Eisenhower, L. B. Johnson, Nixon, Ford, Clinton

PRESIDENTIAL MIX AND MATCH GAME

Type of activity: In this game players try to match dates with the significant events/actions that occurred during a president's term of office (which are found on the time line).

Directions for independent play: Display the time line on a bulletin board or on poster paper located near a table or at a learning center. In a box, have sheets of paper listing five or more events in random order, but no dates. Given a limited time period, the player uses the time line to identify the correct dates for the events. After the player completes the dates for the events, the sheet is turned in and checked for accuracy.

Directions for team play: Prepare cards that show dates in which events occurred, one date per card. Put the date cards in a box. Divide into two teams. Explain that in this game teams will take turns matching events and dates. A correct match earns one point. The team that scores more points wins. Specify a limited period of time for playing the game. Deal out the time lines so that each member of a team has the same number. Randomly select a date card and ask members of one team to check their cards to determine if one of their time lines tells them what occurred on that date. For example, if you say "1863," students would check their time lines to see if they have information about that year. If a player has the correct answer, the team scores a point. Play proceeds when a date is selected for the opposing team to identify.

NAME THE PRESIDENT GAME

Type of activity: a game in which players on teams take turns identifying the last name of a president when given the first name.

Directions: Divide into two teams. Explain that the purpose of the game is to use the president cards to correctly name the presidents. When they are told the first name of a president, they must identify the president's last name. For example, if you say "Thomas," a correct match would be "Jefferson." Deal out president cards to team members. Say the first name of a president, and let members of the first team check their cards to identify the last name. If the team cannot come up with a name, play passes to the other team. Award a team one point for each correct name. Once a president has been named, his name cannot be used again in the game. Continue the game, rotating from one team to another.

PRESIDENTS IN A ROW

Type of activity: An activity in which players place president cards in order from first to most recent.

Directions: Deal out president cards to students. Explain that the purpose of the activity is to arrange the cards in order from the first president to the current president. The cards can be displayed on the chalkboard tray or on the floor or large table. Starting with the first president, each player, in turn, adds his/her card to the display. When a player adds his/her card, he/she can use the information on the card to make a brief oral report about the president.

PAIRING AND SHARING

Type of activity: Students pair up and share information on presidents. This activity requires an open area large enough to accommodate students.

Directions: Divide the class into two groups. Give one president card to each of the students in one group. Give the corresponding presidential time line to each student in the other group.

When you give the signal, students with president card and time line for the same president are to pair up and discuss the information about their president. After sufficient time for discussion has elapsed, let pairs of students hold up their cards and talk about what they have learned about their president.

EVENTS, DATES, AND PRESIDENTS

Type of activity: Students use cards to match events to dates and presidents.

Directions: On the board, chart paper, or an overhead transparency, create a chart like the following:

Event	Date	President

Tell students that their task is to use the president and time lines to help you complete the chart above. Deal out president cards and time lines to students. Explain that you will tell them an important event. They can check their presidential cards and time lines to see if they have information about the date of the event and the president with whom the event is associated. When a student finds the information, he/she can complete the chart by recording the date and president's name. For example, if the event is "Cuban missile crisis occurred," then "1962" and "John F. Kennedy" would be added to the chart under the appropriate headings.

GUESS WHO

Type of activity: This game can be played as a review after students have used the cards to learn facts about the presidents. In this game a player on one team gives clues about a president, and the other team tries to guess the president's name. Play alternately from one team to the other.

Directions: Divide the class into two teams. Deal out the president cards to players. Using one of the president cards he/she is dealt, a player on one team will give a clue (i.e., an important event associated with a president). Players on the other team can confer as they try to guess the name. If they get the name correct on the first clue, the team scores three points. If a team cannot come up with the correct name, a point is scored against the team, and a second clue is given. If the team gets the name correct on the second clue, the team scores two points, but failure to come up with the name results in another one-point loss. If the team gets the name correct on the third clue, the team scores one point, but failure results in another one-point loss. Play passes to the other team, and a player from that team gives a clue and the process is repeated. Play continues, moving from one team to another, for a limited period of time. Once a president has been named, the name cannot be used again in the game. The team that scores more points wins.

INDEPENDENT PRESIDENT CARD ACTIVITY

Type of activity: Individual students use cards to practice information-gathering and writing skills.

Directions: Let individual students choose a president card. There are two tasks. First, have the student make a list of each fact they can find about the president. Then, let them use the list of facts to do any one or more of the following:
  1. Write a classified ad based on the facts.
  2. Create a newspaper article with a headline using the facts.
  3. Create a set of trivia questions based on the facts.
  4. Create a TV infomercial using the facts.
  5. Write an editorial using the facts.

TIME LINE ACTIVITIES

Type of activity: Students use the time line to answer the "time" questions and fill in statements.

Directions: Let students use the time line to answer questions and fill in statements using the format below:
  1. What happened between _____ and _____?

  2. Which event occurred first, _____ or _____?

  3. Put the following events in chronological order _____, _____, and _____.

  4. Can you identify an event that might have caused _____ to happen?

  5. How long ago did _____ happen?

  6. How many years separate these two events? _____ and _____

  7. How many presidents were there from _____ to _____?

  8. How might _____ be related to _____?

  9. If _____ happened, what might happen next?

George Washington

1789	George Washington sworn in as first president
1791	Eli Whitney invents cotton gin
1793	Bill of Rights ratified
1794	Philadelphia is temporary capital
	Whiskey Rebellion

First President
Born: February 22, 1732—Pope's Creek, Virginia
Died: December 14, 1799

Born on his father's estate, George Washington was a fourth-generation American. Taught at home by his family, George liked to read and was very good in math. Early on, he showed a real talent for surveying and making maps. Appointed county surveyor, he explored much of Virginia. Washington's skill at military affairs was honed as a leader in the French and Indian War. After his discharge from the army, he settled down as a gentleman farmer at Mount Vernon and also served as a delegate to the House of Burgesses, Virginia's colonial legislature. Angry about England's treatment of the colonies, Washington spoke out against British rule as a member of the First Continental Congress. When the Revolutionary War broke out, he was elected commander in chief of the American army and led the patriots to victory over the British. After the war Washington played an important role in unifying the country as president of the Constitutional Convention. Once the Constitution was adopted, he became the first president of the United States of America. Words spoken at his funeral sum up how the nation felt about him: "First in war, first in peace, and first in the hearts of his countrymen."

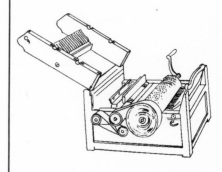

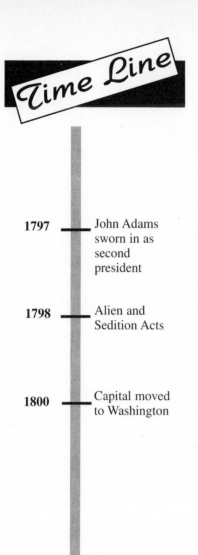
1797	John Adams sworn in as second president
1798	Alien and Sedition Acts
1800	Capital moved to Washington

John Adams

Courtesy Independence National Historical Park

Second President
Party: Federalist
Born: October 30, 1735—Braintree, Massachusetts
Died: July 4, 1826

John Adams was well educated. He graduated from Harvard and taught school briefly before becoming a lawyer. Adams quickly became known in Boston as an outspoken critic of British colonial practices. He relished every act of opposition toward the British, and yet his high principles led him to defend a British soldier charged with murder. Five colonists had been killed in a violent clash that came to be called the "Boston Massacre." John Adams agreed to defend the leader of the British troops that had fired on the colonists because he believed that everyone was entitled to a fair trial. Adams won the case and the soldier was freed. Later, as a delegate to the First Continental Congress, he was a strong advocate for independence. In fact, it was John Adams who wrote a statement adopted by the Congress that declared that England had no right to tell the colonies what to do. At the Second Continental Congress, Adams was one of five persons chosen to work on the Declaration of Independence. During the Revolutionary War, Adams served as a diplomat in Europe. When Adams was president, America faced serious problems with France. Many urged Adams to go to war, but he managed to keep the peace. Although Adams made his political opponents angry, he is admired today for his courage and his deeply held convictions.

Thomas Jefferson

Courtesy Bowdoin College Museum of Art

1801 — Jefferson sworn in as third president

1803 — Louisiana Purchase

1804 — Lewis and Clark Expedition

1807 — Robert Fulton makes first practical steamboat trip

1808 — Slave importation outlawed

Third President
Party: Democratic-Republican
Born: April 13, 1743—Shadwell, Virginia
Died: July 4, 1826

"We hold these truths to be self-evident, that all men are created equal . . ."—Thomas Jefferson expressed his beliefs with those famous words when he wrote the Declaration of Independence in 1776. Jefferson came from a family that valued education. He went to the College of William and Mary in Virginia, where he studied science, mathematics, and law. His interests and talents were many and varied. He played the violin, designed his own home, invented mechanical devices, and enjoyed gardening. Jefferson played a large role in shaping our nation. He was one of Virginia's representatives at the Continental Congress in Philadelphia, which is where he wrote the Declaration of Independence. He succeeded Patrick Henry as Virginia's second governor. Jefferson also served as minister to France, and he became the first secretary of state in President Washington's cabinet. In 1801 Jefferson was sworn in as America's third president. Two of the most significant events during Jefferson's administration were the purchase of the Louisiana Territory and the Lewis and Clark Expedition, sent to explore the vast region. Jefferson thought every citizen should play a role in government. He favored a limited federal government and strong state governments. For Jefferson, education was essential for informed and effective citizenship. One of his proudest accomplishments was founding the University of Virginia.

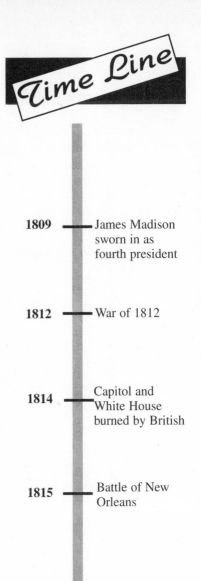

Time Line

1809 — James Madison sworn in as fourth president

1812 — War of 1812

1814 — Capitol and White House burned by British

1815 — Battle of New Orleans

James Madison

Fourth President
Party: Democratic-Republican
Born: March 16, 1751—Port Conway, Virginia
Died: June 28, 1836

James Madison overcame a sickly childhood to become the "Father of the Constitution." The oldest of 12 children, he received his early education from his parents, tutors, and a private school. After graduating from Princeton in 1771, Madison studied for the ministry, but stirred by the growing trouble with Britain and talk of revolution, he soon turned to politics. A brilliant thinker and writer, Madison quickly established himself as a leader of the fight for freedom. He served in the Virginia Convention that met in Williamsburg in 1776 and was a delegate to the Second Continental Congress in 1780. Madison's hard work at the Constitutional Convention of 1787 helped unify the new nation. His records of what happened there, together with the role he played in writing the document, earned him the title of "Father of the Constitution." Madison was also one of the authors of the Federalist Papers. These famous essays helped convince the states to ratify the new constitution. During Jefferson's presidency Madison was secretary of state. Madison was sworn in as president in 1809 and served two terms. During President Madison's administration, the United States fought another war with Britain, the War of 1812. When the British attacked and burned Washington in 1814, Madison had to flee the capital.

James Monroe

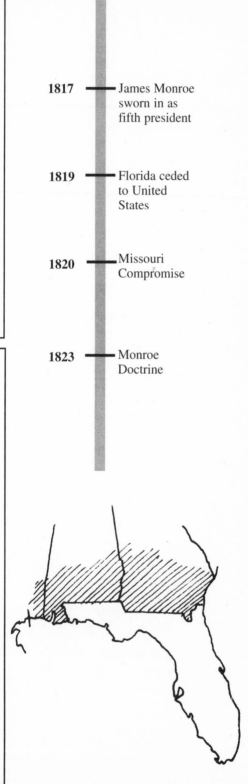

1817 — James Monroe sworn in as fifth president

1819 — Florida ceded to United States

1820 — Missouri Compromise

1823 — Monroe Doctrine

Fifth President
Party: Democratic-Republican
Born: April 28, 1758—Westmoreland County, Virginia
Died: July 4, 1831

The son of a rich planter, young James Monroe was educated by tutors and in private school. After attending the College of William and Mary a few months, Monroe abruptly quit school to join the army and fight in the Revolutionary War. After the war Monroe studied law with Thomas Jefferson, who became his lifelong friend and advisor. Monroe wanted a bill of rights to protect individual liberties added to the new constitution, and he refused to support the constitution's ratification without it. Throughout his life Monroe was very active in politics. He was elected to the Senate, appointed to serve as minister to France and Britain, and elected governor of Virginia twice. Monroe was an aggressive statesman and spoke his views forcefully. Among his many important political accomplishments before becoming president were his successful negotiations with France to secure the Louisiana Purchase. President Monroe was a popular leader and especially strong in foreign affairs. He obtained Florida and settled the border disagreements with Britain over Canada. His greatest foreign policy achievement was named for him—the Monroe Doctrine. The Monroe Doctrine declared that European colonization in the Western Hemisphere must stop.

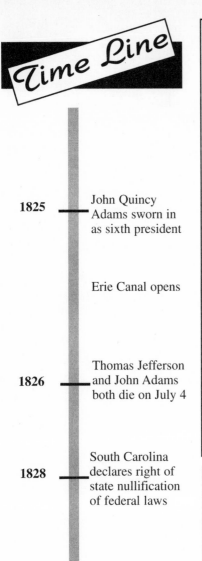

1825 — John Quincy Adams sworn in as sixth president

Erie Canal opens

1826 — Thomas Jefferson and John Adams both die on July 4

1828 — South Carolina declares right of state nullification of federal laws

John Quincy Adams

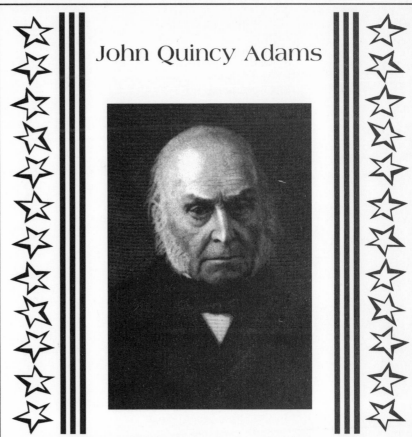

Sixth President
Party: Democratic-Republican
Born: July 11, 1767—Braintree, Massachusetts
Died: February 23, 1848

John Quincy Adams was a bright child. He attended private schools in the United States and in Europe when he traveled with his diplomat-father abroad. He graduated from Harvard, became a lawyer, and also wrote about politics. In 1803 he was elected to the Senate. He served as a diplomat in Europe for three presidents. Through his childhood associations, he became a linguist and well informed on many subjects. He was a capable secretary of state under President Monroe. In fact, Adams was responsible for many of Monroe's foreign accomplishments, including the negotiations that led to the acquisition of Florida from Spain. Adams barely won the presidency in the deadlocked election of 1824. Because he failed to receive a majority of votes from the electoral college, Adams was elected president by the House of Representatives. Despite a lively campaign, Adams lost to Andrew Jackson in his bid for a second term. Adams did not retire from politics, however. Instead, he was elected to the House of Representatives, where he served for 17 years. In Congress he spoke out against slavery and war with Mexico. Adams was in Congress debating an issue when he had a stroke. He died two days later.

Andrew Jackson

Courtesy Metropolitan Museum of Art, Dick Fund

Time Line

1829 — Andrew Jackson sworn in as seventh president

1831 — Nat Turner leads slave rebellion

1832 — Black Hawk War

1836 — Texan defenders of the Alamo killed

Seventh President
Party: Democratic
Born: March 15, 1767—Waxhaw District, South Carolina
Died: June 8, 1845

Andrew Jackson's life reads like an adventure novel. He was the first president born in a log cabin. His father died before he was born. At age 13 he joined the militia and fought in the Revolutionary War. The scar on his forehead came when he refused to obey his captors. Jackson settled in Tennessee at an early age and quickly made a name for himself in Tennessee politics. He had a reputation of being tough and was nicknamed "Old Hickory." Jackson overcame a limited education to become a self-made man. He served Tennessee as a prosecuting attorney, a member of the House of Representatives, and a U.S. senator. During the War of 1812, Jackson became a national hero after he won a huge victory over the British at the Battle of New Orleans. His military fame helped propel him to the presidency in the election of 1828. He was especially popular in the West and South. Jackson's administration was filled with controversy. He replaced many government workers with people who supported his election—a practice that became known as the spoils system. Jackson declared war on the powerful Bank of the United States and worked successfully to end its influence over the national economy. In a controversy over tariffs, he fought to preserve the Union when he forced South Carolina to obey federal laws. Although he had many opponents, Jackson was a strong leader who had the courage and tenacity to use the powers of the presidency to the fullest.

Time Line

1837 — Martin Van Buren sworn in as eighth president

1838 — Cherokees removed to Oklahoma in "Trail of Tears"

1840 — William Lloyd Garrison supporters vote to admit women to American Antislavery Society

Martin Van Buren

Eighth President
Party: Democratic
Born: December 5, 1782—Kinderhook, New York
Died: July 24, 1862

Martin Van Buren's father farmed and was an innkeeper. Young Martin met and listened to the politicians who stopped at the inn on their way to and from the state capital. He attended village schools and then focused his study on law. At age 14 he was a law clerk, and by the age of 21 he had a successful law practice. Van Buren had strong political ambitions. He was nicknamed "Little Magician" because of his political skills and small size. Active in New York politics, Van Buren was a state attorney general and a state senator before his election to the U.S. Senate in 1821. He helped Andrew Jackson win the presidency, and as a reward Jackson appointed him secretary of state. He was vice president during Jackson's second term. Soon after Van Buren's own election to the presidency in 1836, his troubles began. A nationwide depression caused financial panic. There were also accusations that Van Buren was an "aristocrat" who had little concern for the common man. Van Buren's popularity plummeted and he was defeated in his bid for a second term. He failed again for the presidency in 1848 when he ran on the Free Soil Party ticket.

William Henry Harrison

Courtesy Metropolitan Museum of Art, Stokes-Hawes Collection

1841 — William Henry Harrison sworn in as ninth president on March 4

He dies of pneumonia on April 4

April 10—the New York *Tribune* began publication

Ninth President
Party: Whig
Born: February 9, 1773—Charles City County, Virginia
Died: April 4, 1841

William Henry Harrison's presidency is the shortest on record—it lasted 31 days. After giving a long inauguration speech in bitter cold weather, he caught pneumonia and died. Although born in Virginia, Harrison made a name for himself as a frontier administrator and Indian fighter in what is now Indiana. He was appointed secretary of the Northwest Territory and also represented the Territory in Congress. Later, he was appointed governor of the Indiana Territory and served as superintendent of Indian affairs. In 1811 he was victorious against the Indians at the Battle of Tippecanoe. Harrison also fought in the War of 1812. After the war, he farmed, was a state and U.S. senator, and a diplomat. He was unsuccessful in his run for the presidency in 1836, but in 1840 he won on the slogan "Tippecanoe and Tyler too." During the "Log Cabin" campaign, Harrison was portrayed as a common, cider-drinking man in an effort to appeal to back country folk. Yet this description did not agree with the facts: Harrison was actually born into one of Virginia's wealthiest families. His father was one of the signers of the Declaration of Independence.

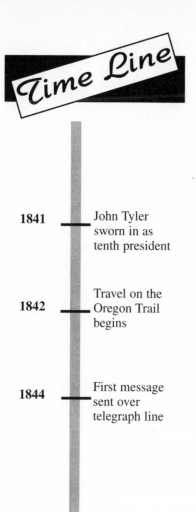

1841 — John Tyler sworn in as tenth president

1842 — Travel on the Oregon Trail begins

1844 — First message sent over telegraph line

John Tyler

Tenth President
Party: Whig
Born: March 29, 1790—Charles City County, Virginia
Died: January 18, 1862

John Tyler was born into a prominent Virginia family. His father was a governor of Virginia. He went to private school as a youth and graduated from the College of William and Mary. He studied law with his father and then followed him into politics. Tyler's party affiliation changed over the course of his career. Originally a Democratic-Republican, he held both state and national offices before he was put on the Whig ticket as vice president in the election of 1840. When President Harrison died a few weeks after his inauguration, Tyler found he could not agree with the Whig policies. He had opposing views about national banks, tariffs, federally financed projects, and slavery. True to his convictions, Tyler vetoed Whig bills and worked hard to get his own policies passed through Congress. The Whigs considered Tyler a traitor and ousted him from the party. Despite these conflicts, Tyler accomplished some of his goals: settlement laws were passed, trade with China was established, the second Seminole War was ended, and the path was paved for the eventual annexation of Texas. When the Whigs met to choose their candidate for president in the election of 1844, Tyler was of course passed over. Tyler retired from politics at the end of his first term. In 1860 he did vote in favor of Virginia's leaving the Union at the state secession convention.

James K. Polk

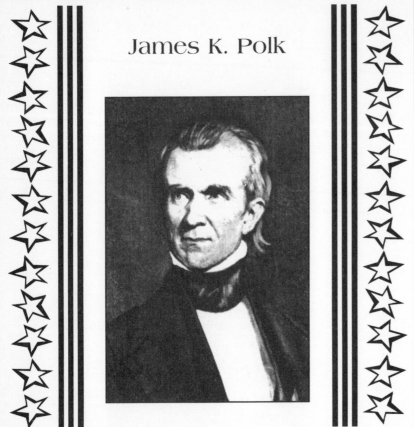

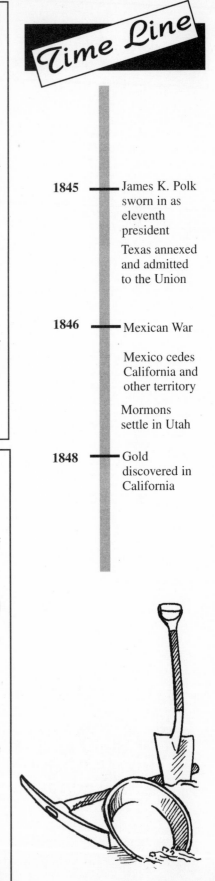

1845 — James K. Polk sworn in as eleventh president

Texas annexed and admitted to the Union

1846 — Mexican War

Mexico cedes California and other territory

Mormons settle in Utah

1848 — Gold discovered in California

Eleventh President
Party: Democratic
Born: Nov. 2, 1795—Mecklenburg County, North Carolina
Died: June 15, 1849

James Polk was the eldest of ten children. Because of childhood health problems, young James was spared from doing his share of farm chores. Despite little formal education as a youth, Polk had a studious nature, and he graduated from the University of North Carolina in 1818. He then studied law, but politics proved more exciting to him than practicing law. Polk held a number of state and national offices. He served in the Tennessee state legislature, U.S. House of Representatives, U.S. Senate, and as governor of Tennessee. Nominated at the Democratic Presidential Convention on the ninth ballot, Polk became the first dark horse candidate to run and then win the presidency. In political parlance, a "dark horse" is a candidate whose chances of winning are supposed to be very poor. Polk wanted to increase the size of the United States. He supported the annexation of Texas and gained California and New Mexico through the Mexican War. Polk also settled the dispute with Britain over the Oregon Territory's border with Canada. In the process, he retained American control over present-day Oregon and Washington. Today Polk is remembered as a strong-willed president who accomplished much of what he set out to do. At the time, many Americans believed in Manifest Destiny, which is the belief that the United States had the right to conquer and settle America from sea to sea. True to his word, Polk kept his campaign promise and did not seek a second term.

1849 — Zachary Taylor sworn in as twelfth president

Harriet Tubman escapes from slavery

1850 — President Taylor dies of an illness in office

Zachary Taylor

Twelfth President
Party: Whig
Born: November 24, 1784—Orange County, Virginia
Died: July 9, 1850

Zachary Taylor grew up on the family farm near the Kentucky frontier. There were no schools, so he studied with tutors. While still in his teens, Taylor joined the army. A soldier's life appealed to him, and he made the military his career. Taylor served 40 years and fought in the War of 1812, Indian wars, and the Mexican War. During the Mexican War, General Taylor's victory over General Santa Anna and his Mexican troops at Buena Vista made him a national hero. His military exploits gained him the nickname, "Old Rough and Ready." The Whigs recognized Taylor's popularity and drafted him as their nominee for president. He was the first military leader to become president without holding a political office previously. During Taylor's term in office (only 16 months), a crisis was developing over the issue of slavery and the extension of slavery into the newly acquired western land. California had applied to enter the Union as a free state. But if it did, it would upset the existing balance of 15 slave and 15 free states. Congress debated the issue and compromises were proposed, but Taylor did not live to see the outcome. He died in office, and his successor signed the compromise bills into law.

Millard Fillmore

1850 — Millard Fillmore sworn in as thirteenth president

Compromise of 1850

1852 — *Uncle Tom's Cabin* published

Thirteenth President
Party: Whig
Born: January 7, 1800—Cayuga County, New York
Died: March 8, 1874

Millard Fillmore had limited formal education. When he was 14, he became an apprentice to a clothmaker until he decided to study law. He was elected to several state offices and to the U.S. House of Representatives. He succeeded to the presidency after Zachary Taylor's death in 1850. President Fillmore inherited the political crisis over the issue of extending slavery into the newly acquired western lands that had erupted during Taylor's short term. Fillmore backed the compromise bills introduced in Congress by Senator Henry Clay. These bills, when signed into law by Fillmore, became known as the Compromise of 1850. The Compromise allowed California to enter the Union as a free state; but it opened the door for slavery in the new western territories, and it imposed a new fugitive slave law on the North. During Fillmore's presidency, he worked for the expansion of the railroads, sent Commodore Matthew C. Perry to Japan to establish trade and diplomatic relations, and reduced the five-cent stamp to three cents. Angry about Fillmore's attitude toward slavery, the Whigs did not choose him to be their standard bearer in the election of 1852. Instead, they nominated General Winfield Scott, a hero of the Mexican War, who lost the general election. After his term was over, Fillmore resumed his practice of law in Buffalo, New York. In 1856 Fillmore was nominated for president, but was soundly defeated by James Buchanan.

UNCLE TOM'S CABIN

Harriet Beecher Stowe

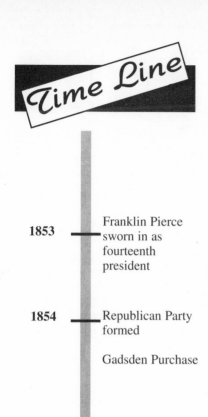

Time Line

1853 — Franklin Pierce sworn in as fourteenth president

1854 — Republican Party formed

Gadsden Purchase

Franklin Pierce

Fourteenth President
Party: Democratic
Born: Nov. 23, 1804—Hillsborough, New Hampshire
Died: October 8, 1869

Franklin Pierce went to a local school until age 11. Then he attended private schools and Bowdin College. He studied law and became an attorney in 1827. He began his political career at an early age. He was elected to the New Hampshire state legislature while still in his mid-20s. Next, he moved on to the U.S. House of Representatives and then to the U.S. Senate. During the Mexican War, he enlisted in the army and attained the rank of brigadier general. After the war he resumed his law practice until he was nominated for president on the forty-ninth ballot. In the election of 1852 Pierce soundly defeated his rival, General Winfield Scott. President Pierce hoped that he could unify the country, but that was not to be. The slavery dispute was at the boiling point, and attitudes were hardening along sectional lines. The times demanded a strong leader, but instead Pierce seemed to make things worse. Pierce's popularity nose-dived with his signing of the Kansas-Nebraska Act, which allowed the spread of slavery into the territories. Also unpopular with Northerners was his interest in acquiring Cuba and his sponsorship of a southern transcontinental railroad. Rejected by his own party and denied the opportunity to run for a second term, Pierce returned home to New Hampshire full of bitterness.

James Buchanan

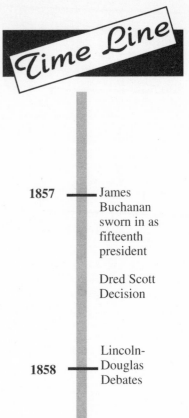

1857 — James Buchanan sworn in as fifteenth president

Dred Scott Decision

1858 — Lincoln-Douglas Debates

1859 — John Brown's raid at Harpers Ferry

1860 — Pony Express started

Fifteenth President
Party: Democratic
Born: April 23, 1791—Cove Gap, Pennsylvania
Died: June 1, 1868

James Buchanan was born in a log cabin. Buchanan learned arithmetic while working in his father's store. His pastor taught him Greek and Latin. He graduated from college in 1809 and then studied law. Buchanan had a good law practice and success in business due in part to his early training. He volunteered to fight in the War of 1812. The rest of his life was spent in public service. He was elected to the Pennsylvania state legislature, U.S. House of Representatives, and U.S. Senate. Buchanan also served as minister to Russia and Great Britain. During President Polk's administration, he served as secretary of state. In the election of 1856 the Democrats nominated Buchanan and he won. In the campaign, the Democrats supported the Compromise of 1850 and the Kansas-Nebraska Act. However, President Buchanan's own views appeared inconsistent and his actions indecisive. Without clear direction, the nation drifted steadily towards war. In 1860 the Democrats split into Northern and Southern groups, and neither wanted Buchanan to be its candidate. The Northern Democrats were led by Stephen Douglas and the Southern Democrats by John Breckinridge. After Lincoln was elected, but not yet inaugurated, seven states seceded from the Union and set up the Confederacy. Buchanan retired to his home in Pennsylvania and remained a supporter of the Union.

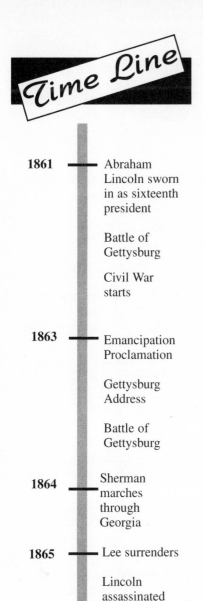

Time Line

1861 — Abraham Lincoln sworn in as sixteenth president

Battle of Gettysburg

Civil War starts

1863 — Emancipation Proclamation

Gettysburg Address

Battle of Gettysburg

1864 — Sherman marches through Georgia

1865 — Lee surrenders

Lincoln assassinated

Abraham Lincoln

Sixteenth President
Party: Republican
Born: February 12, 1809—Hardin County, Kentucky
Died: April 15, 1865

Born in a log cabin and self-educated, Abraham Lincoln went on to lead the nation through the Civil War and preserve the Union. Lincoln moved to New Salem, Illinois, when he was a young man. He worked as a shopkeeper, was postmaster of New Salem, and won a seat in the state legislature before completing his study of the law. Before he entered national politics, Lincoln honed his legal skills riding the circuit on horseback, trying cases in small towns and villages. As a representative to Congress, he was against slavery in new territories, but felt the government should not interfere with it where it already existed. In 1856 Lincoln joined the newly-formed Republican Party and ran against Stephen Douglas for the U.S. Senate. The two candidates engaged in a series of debates held at different cities around the state. Although he lost the election, Lincoln attracted national attention for his well-reasoned and earnest arguments against slavery. After Lincoln was elected president, 11 Southern states seceded from the Union. The Civil War broke out when Confederate forces attacked Ft. Sumter in 1861. In 1863 Lincoln issued the Emancipation Proclamation, which freed the slaves in the states then in rebellion. A few days after Lee's surrender to Grant to end the war, Lincoln was assassinated. It was left to his successor, Andrew Johnson, to carry out his postwar policies.

Andrew Johnson

1865 — Andrew Johnson sworn in as seventeenth president

Thirteenth Amendment abolishes slavery

1866 — Ku Klux Klan formed

1867 — Alaska sold to United States

The Grange organized

1868 — Johnson's impeachment trial

Seventeenth President
Party: National Union Party (a coalition of Republicans and War Democrats)
Born: December 29, 1808—Raleigh, North Carolina
Died: July 31, 1875

Andrew Johnson was born in North Carolina. Like Lincoln, he was a self-educated man. His father died when Andrew was very young. He became an apprentice to a tailor but eventually left that trade and moved to eastern Tennessee. Johnson became a moderately successful businessperson and was active in local politics. He held many important offices including Tennessee state legislator, representative to Congress, U.S. senator, and governor of Tennessee. Although he came from the South and owned slaves, Johnson sided with the common man and disliked the rich plantation owners. He was against the breakup of the Union. When Tennessee seceded, Johnson was the only Southern senator to stay in Washington. After the Civil War broke out, President Lincoln appointed Johnson military governor of Tennessee. Lincoln chose Johnson as a running mate in the election of 1864. After Lincoln's assassination, Johnson became president. He tried to implement Lincoln's plans for Reconstruction, or rebuilding the South, but Radical Republicans in Congress disapproved. He was impeached by the House of Representatives on questionable charges, but the Senate failed by one vote to convict him. Johnson remained active in politics after his presidency and was applauded when he returned to Washington as a member of the U.S. Senate.

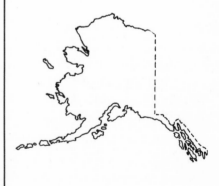

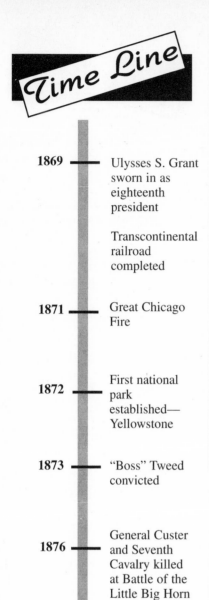

1869	Ulysses S. Grant sworn in as eighteenth president
	Transcontinental railroad completed
1871	Great Chicago Fire
1872	First national park established— Yellowstone
1873	"Boss" Tweed convicted
1876	General Custer and Seventh Cavalry killed at Battle of the Little Big Horn

Ulysses S. Grant

Courtesy Peter A. Juley & Son

Eighteenth President
Party: Republican
Born: April 27, 1822—Point Pleasant, Ohio
Died: July 23, 1885

Raised on a farm, Ulysses Grant did not like doing farm chores, nor did he enjoy helping in his father's tannery. His only real fondness was for horses. After graduating from West Point, he served as an officer in the army and fought in the Mexican War. After the war, he left the military and tried to support his family by farming and through various business ventures, but he was not very successful. When the Civil War started, he rejoined the army and was put in command of a Union infantry unit. Grant boldly took the offensive and scored a series of victories over the Confederates in Tennessee and Mississippi. Because of his military successes in the West, Grant was eventually put in charge of all the Union armies. On April 9, 1865, General Lee surrendered to General Grant at Appomattox Court House in Virginia to end the war. The Republicans nominated Grant for president, and he easily won the election of 1868. However, some of his appointees were not honest, and his administration was marred by scandals and corruption. Grant's later years were spent writing his autobiography, which was finished a few days before he died.

Rutherford B. Hayes

Courtesy Library of Congress, Brady-Handy Collection

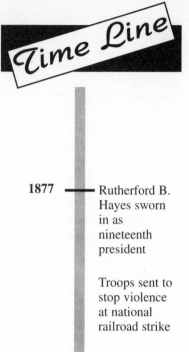

1877 — Rutherford B. Hayes sworn in as nineteenth president

Troops sent to stop violence at national railroad strike

1878 — Thomas Edison founded Edison Electric Light Co.

1879 — First F. W. Woolworth store opened

Nineteenth President
Party: Republican
Born: October 4, 1822—Delaware, Ohio
Died: January 17, 1893

Rutherford B. Hayes was raised by his uncle and received a good education. He graduated from Kenyon College and Harvard Law School. He was a successful criminal lawyer and served in the Civil War. Hayes distinguished himself in the war: he was wounded several times and promoted to the rank of major general. He was elected to the U.S. House of Representatives while still fighting in the war, but did not take his seat until after he was discharged from the army. He went on to serve two terms as governor of Ohio. He was the Republican nominee for president in the election of 1876. The election was so close that a special electoral commission appointed by Congress had to resolve some disputed electoral votes. Hayes ended up winning the election by one electoral vote. During Hayes' administration, the era of Reconstruction was ended with the withdrawal of federal troops from the South. In the aftermath of Grant's corrupt administration, Hayes supported civil service reforms. He also sent troops to stop rioting and violence during a national railroad strike. Hayes kept his promise to the voters that he would not run for a second term. He returned home to Ohio where he was active in several humanitarian causes until his death.

Time Line

1881 — James A. Garfield sworn in as twentieth president

Garfield assassinated

Tuskegee Institute established

James A. Garfield

Courtesy National Archives, Brady Collection

Twentieth President
Party: Republican
Born: November 19, 1831—Orange, Ohio
Died: September 19, 1881

When James Garfield was just a small child, his father died. The family had a hard time making ends meet. Garfield worked on the family farm and at odd jobs to earn money. Despite his difficult circumstances, Garfield managed to get a good education. He graduated from college, taught, and studied law. He also fought courageously in the Civil War and rose to the rank of major general. He had shown an interest in politics before the war, and in 1862 he was elected to the U.S. House of Representatives while still in the army. He served nine terms in Congress. At first he joined with the Radical Republicans in Congress and wanted to punish the defeated South harshly, but later he became more lenient. In 1880 he was nominated for president on the sixth ballot. Garfield won the general election. The old spoils system was still in effect, and President Garfield appointed several of his supporters to government positions. On July 2, 1881, a disappointed office-seeker shot him as he was entering a train station. Garfield died in September. Garfield's assassination prompted Congress to get rid of the spoils system and create a civil service system.

Chester A. Arthur

Courtesy New-York Historical Society

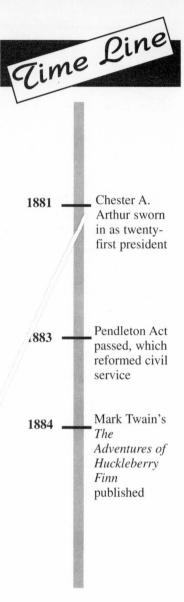

1881 — Chester A. Arthur sworn in as twenty-first president

1883 — Pendleton Act passed, which reformed civil service

1884 — Mark Twain's *The Adventures of Huckleberry Finn* published

Twenty-first President
Party: Republican
Born: October 5, 1829—Fairfield, Vermont
Died: November 18, 1886

Chester Arthur attended many schools because his father's pastoral duties required the family to move frequently. After graduation from college, Arthur studied law, and then set up a practice in New York City. In one case, he successfully defended a fugitive slave. He became involved with the start of the Republican Party, and he was a firm supporter of machine politics and the spoils system. In fact, he benefitted greatly from them. He readily accepted political positions in exchange for political favors done. During the Civil War, Arthur was in the state militia in administrative positions. Arthur became a bitter enemy of President Hayes and the reform Republicans for forcing him to resign from an important position given to him during Grant's corrupt presidency. Arthur was nominated as Garfield's running mate because of his strong party loyalty. Much to the surprise of party leaders, when Arthur succeeded to the presidency, he did not make political appointments under the spoils system. Instead, he signed the Civil Service Act that eliminated such appointments! Arthur knew he had a fatal illness, which he kept secret. After completing his term in 1885, he retired to New York. He died in November of the following year.

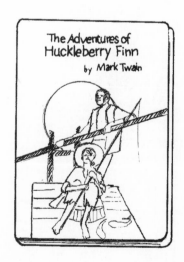

The Adventures of Huckleberry Finn by Mark Twain

1885	Grover Cleveland sworn in as twenty-second president
1886	Presidential Succession Act passed
	Haymarket Riot
	Statue of Liberty
1887	Election Count Act
	Interstate Commerce Act
1893	Cleveland sworn in as twenty-fourth president
	Financial Panic
1894	Pullman Strike
1896	*Plessy v. Ferguson*

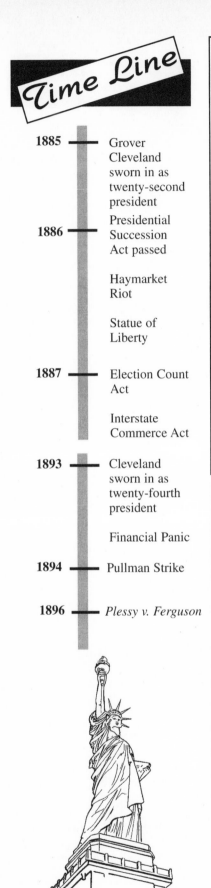

Grover Cleveland

Twenty-second and Twenty-fourth President
Party: Democratic
Born: March 18, 1837—Caldwell, New Jersey
Died: June 24, 1908

At age 14 Grover Cleveland quit school so that he could work to help support his family. Although he did not attend college, he studied law and became an attorney. He was attracted to politics, and worked his way up through a number of local and state offices, culminating in his election as governor of New York in 1882. In 1884, as calls for political reform increased, the Democrats nominated Cleveland, who had a reputation for honesty and high principles, as their candidate for president. After a nasty, name-calling campaign, Cleveland emerged the winner. He was the first Democrat to be elected president in 28 years. As president, Cleveland took a firm stand on civil service reform, conservation of resources, and election reform. Cleveland lost his attempt to be reelected in 1888, but fours years later he tried again and was reelected in 1892. He is the only president to serve two, nonconsecutive terms. During his second term, Cleveland had to deal with a host of problems. One of the worst was the financial panic of 1893. It started when the stock market plunged and led to the shutdown of thousands of businesses and to the elimination of millions of jobs. Unable to solve all of these problems, Cleveland did not seek another term.

Benjamin Harrison

Courtesy Benjamin H. Walker

1889	Benjamin Harrison sworn in as twenty-third president
1890	Battle of Wounded Knee
	Sherman Antitrust Act
1891	Forest Reserve Act
1892	Ellis Island receives immigrants
	Homestead Strike

Twenty-third President
Party: Republican
Born: August 20, 1833—North Bend, Ohio
Died: March 13, 1901

Benjamin Harrison was born into a very patriotic and political family. He was the great-grandson of a signer of the Declaration of Independence and the grandson of the ninth president. His father was also a politician. Harrison's early education was with tutors. After graduation from Miami University in Ohio, he studied law and became a prominent lawyer. Following in the family tradition, he began to become involved in politics, working for the Republican Party. After serving with distinction as an officer in the Civil War, Harrison decided to run for political office. He lost his bid to become governor of Ohio but was elected to the U.S. Senate. By 1888 Harrison had become known not only because of the family name, but also for his own accomplishments as a soldier, lawyer, and politician. The Republicans nominated him for president and he won the election, even though he did not win the popular vote. As president, Harrison was strong on foreign affairs. He built a two-ocean navy, negotiated trade policies, and created the Pan American Union. He let domestic affairs follow party lines and congressional leadership. His attitudes toward taxes, pensions, and trusts probably cost him the election in 1892. After finishing his term, he practiced law and wrote.

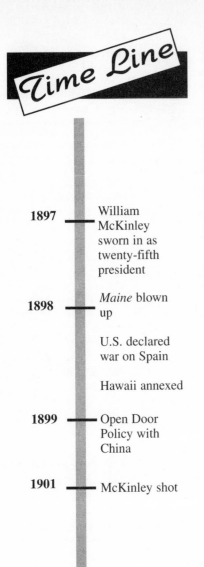

Time Line

- **1897** — William McKinley sworn in as twenty-fifth president
- **1898** — *Maine* blown up

  U.S. declared war on Spain

  Hawaii annexed
- **1899** — Open Door Policy with China
- **1901** — McKinley shot

William McKinley

Twenty-fifth President
Party: Republican
Born: January 29, 1843—Niles, Ohio
Died: September 14, 1901

William McKinley went to local and private schools before attending college. McKinley fought in a number of battles during the Civil War and was promoted to the rank of brigadier general. After serving in the war, he studied law. Not content with just practicing law, McKinley knew from an early age that he wanted to be president. He served two terms in the U.S. House of Representatives and two terms as governor of Ohio. In 1896 the Republicans chose McKinley to be their presidential candidate. He refused to travel during the campaign because of his invalid wife, so trainloads of people traveled to his home to hear him speak from his front porch. In contrast, his opponent, William Jennings Bryan, spent 14 weeks on the campaign trail, making speeches in 27 states. McKinley won the election with the first popular vote majority since 1872. During McKinley's term, the Spanish-American War was fought, and the United States acquired Guam, Puerto Rico, and the Philippines in the peace settlement. Domestically, McKinley was in favor of high tariffs to protect American goods, and he also favored the Gold Standard, which meant that the U.S. government would back its paper money with gold. Six months after his second term began, McKinley was shot while attending the Pan American Exposition in Buffalo, New York. He died a few days later.

Theodore Roosevelt

Time Line

1901 — Theodore Roosevelt sworn in as twenty-sixth president

1903 — Panama Canal Treaty

Wright brothers flight at Kitty Hawk

1906 — San Francisco earthquake

Pure Food & Drug Act

1908 — Model T Ford introduced

Twenty-sixth President
Party: Republican
Born: October 27, 1858—New York, New York
Died: January 6, 1919

Theodore Roosevelt was an energetic yet sickly child with a curious mind. He was taught by private tutors. Roosevelt graduated from Harvard in 1880. Being a lawyer did not interest him, but public service did. At the age of 23, he was elected to the New York state legislature. Roosevelt loved the outdoors, and after both his mother and first wife died, he spent two years roughing it in the Dakota Territory. He held several appointed offices after he returned home. He became a national hero as leader of a calvary regiment called the "Rough Riders." Their successful attack near San Juan Hill in Cuba was reported in all the newspapers. Elected governor of New York in 1898, Roosevelt was a vigorous opponent of the spoils system and other corrupt practices. His reform efforts did not please some party leaders, so they came up with a way to get him out of the state: Send him to Washington. Two years after being elected governor, Roosevelt was McKinley's vice president. Among Roosevelt's many accomplishments as president was breaking up corrupt business trusts, preserving forest land, and the start of the Panama Canal. He did not seek another term in 1908; however, he did run again in 1912 but lost. A man of many talents, Roosevelt traveled, wrote books, and stayed involved in politics until the day he died.

Time Line

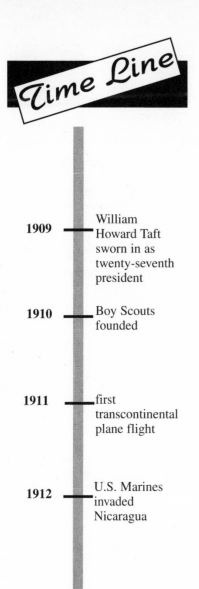

1909 — William Howard Taft sworn in as twenty-seventh president

1910 — Boy Scouts founded

1911 — first transcontinental plane flight

1912 — U.S. Marines invaded Nicaragua

William Howard Taft

Courtesy Library of Congress

Twenty-seventh President
Party: Republican
Born: September 15, 1857—Cincinnati, Ohio
Died: March 8, 1930

William Taft was a member of a prominent Republican family. His father had served in important positions in both Grant's and Arthur's administrations. Taft was well educated, with degrees from Yale and Cincinnati Law School. He spent 20 years of his life practicing law and serving as a judge. He also served as first civil governor for the Philippines and as secretary of war in Theodore Roosevelt's cabinet. When President Theodore Roosevelt announced he would not seek another term, he hand-picked Taft to run for the office. After Taft won the election of 1908, he successfully pursued many of Roosevelt's policies, including busting business trusts and political reform. However, many progressives, including Roosevelt, did not like the way he was handling tariffs and conservation matters. In the election of 1912 they decided to run against Taft on the "Bull Moose" ticket, with Roosevelt as their candidate. This third-party tactic split the Republican vote, and they both lost the election to the Democratic candidate, Woodrow Wilson. Taft returned to his law practice until he was appointed as chief justice to the Supreme Court. He is the only person to have served as both president and chief justice.

Woodrow Wilson

Courtesy New-York Historical Society

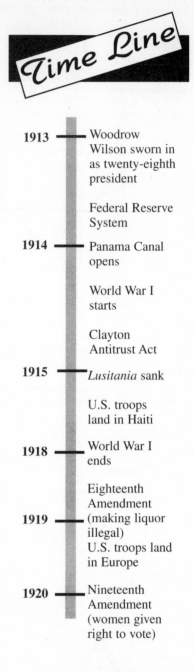

1913 — Woodrow Wilson sworn in as twenty-eighth president

Federal Reserve System

1914 — Panama Canal opens

World War I starts

Clayton Antitrust Act

1915 — *Lusitania* sank

U.S. troops land in Haiti

1918 — World War I ends

Eighteenth Amendment (making liquor illegal)

1919 — U.S. troops land in Europe

1920 — Nineteenth Amendment (women given right to vote)

Twenty-eighth President
Party: Democratic
Born: December 29, 1856—Stanton, Virginia
Died: February 3, 1924

Woodrow Wilson was born into a family that valued a good education. An excellent student, he graduated from Princeton University, the University of Virginia Law School, and Johns Hopkins University, where he received his doctorate in political science. He taught at several colleges and was recognized for his lecturing skills. Both scholarly and popular, he was selected president of Princeton in 1902 and seemed like the perfect candidate for governor. The New Jersey political bosses wanted him to run because they thought he would leave their powerful political machine alone. Once elected, however, Wilson proved them wrong and from the start supported progressive reforms. The governor's political housekeeping in New Jersey got the nation's attention, and he was chosen by the Democrats as their candidate in the 1912 election. Wilson won the election because of the split Republican ticket. During his first term, he fought for reform and aggressively pursued his idealistic views. That, along with keeping the nation out of war, was enough to win him a second term. However, three months later the United States was at war. After the war Wilson worked for peace, but he suffered a stroke which made him an invalid. He remained in office, but his wife and doctors secretly carried out many of his duties.

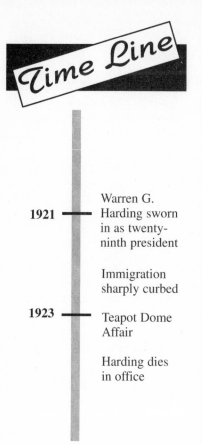

1921 — Warren G. Harding sworn in as twenty-ninth president

Immigration sharply curbed

1923 — Teapot Dome Affair

Harding dies in office

Warren G. Harding

Courtesy Library of Congress

Twenty-ninth President
Party: Republican
Born: November 2, 1865—Corsico, Ohio
Died: August 2, 1923

Warren Harding attended college, taught, studied law, and sold insurance before he settled on a career in publishing. Through his newspaper, he became known throughout the state. Encouraged to enter politics, he was first elected to the state senate and then lieutenant governor. Failing in a run for governor, he was elected to the U.S. Senate in 1914. In the Senate, Harding fought against joining Wilson's League of Nations but supported women's right to vote. In 1920 he was nominated by the Republicans for the presidency. The nation, weary of war and reform, welcomed Harding's call for a return to "normalcy," and he won the election easily. Harding relied on his cabinet and Congress to run the government; he preferred to play poker with his buddies. Unfortunately, some of the friends he appointed proved to be corrupt and used their offices for personal gain. When their criminal activities were revealed, two of them committed suicide and others were sent to jail. In an effort to regain the nation's confidence in his administration, Harding made a train trip across the country. He became ill on the West Coast and died in San Francisco, California, on August 2, 1923. Despite the scandals, there was a great outpouring of grief from the American people on the news of the president's death.

Calvin Coolidge

Courtesy Library of Congress

Thirtieth President
Party: Republican
Born: July 4, 1872—Plymouth, Vermont
Died: January 5, 1933

Calvin Coolidge was raised on a Vermont farm and attended a one-room school. He graduated from Amherst College in 1895. After college, he studied law and soon became active in politics. He held many local and state offices, including mayor, state senator, lieutenant governor, and governor. He was the opposite of the outgoing Harding. He earned the nickname "Silent Cal" because he was a man of few words and seldom smiled. He was the first vice president to attend cabinet meetings. When Harding died, Coolidge was awakened at his father's farm and told the news. After dressing, he was sworn in by his father— and then he went back to bed! Coolidge had a reputation for honesty, and he cleaned up the messy scandals of Harding's administration. Like Harding, he believed that government should not interfere with big business. Government programs to help ordinary citizens were ignored. In 1924 he won the presidential election in his own right using the slogan "Keep Cool with Coolidge." He chose not to run in 1928 and said, "Good-bye, I've had a very nice time in Washington."

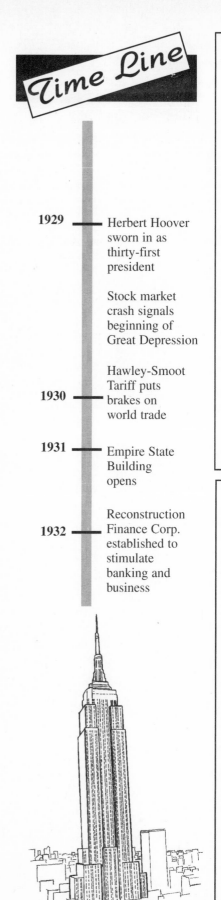

Time Line

1929 — Herbert Hoover sworn in as thirty-first president

Stock market crash signals beginning of Great Depression

Hawley-Smoot Tariff puts brakes on world trade

1930 —

1931 — Empire State Building opens

1932 — Reconstruction Finance Corp. established to stimulate banking and business

Herbert Hoover

Courtesy Library of Congress

Thirty-first President
Party: Republican
Born: August 10, 1874—West Branch, Iowa
Died: October 20, 1964

Herbert Hoover's childhood was not easy. Both his parents died by the time he was nine. He was raised by relatives, and his early education was spotty. Hoover was an intelligent and energetic individual, however, and graduated from college with a degree in mining engineering. He made a fortune developing mines all over the world. A brilliant manager, Hoover headed the U.S. Food Administration and U.S. Department of Commerce before becoming president. He directed a food-relief program for Europe and organized trade associations and developed more efficient business practices. Hoover's skills were recognized by the Republican Party, and he was nominated for president in 1928. Campaigning on a pro-business platform, he won in a landslide victory. Political storms gathered quickly, however. Eight months after he took office, the stock market plunged the last week of October in 1929. Hoover's response to the Great Depression was to call for voluntary and local actions. But the Depression deepened, and Hoover lost the election of 1932. Hoover had many active years after he left office. He was an author, humanitarian, and advisor to presidents. Hoover was also very generous with the money he had made in business, and he contributed to many charitable projects.

Franklin D. Roosevelt

Courtesy Library of Congress

1933 — Franklin D. Roosevelt sworn in as thirty-second president

New Deal begins

1935 — Social Security Act

1941 — Pearl Harbor

1945 — Roosevelt dies in office

Thirty-second President
Party: Democratic
Born: January 30, 1882—Hyde Park, New York
Died: April 12, 1945

Franklin D. Roosevelt was born into a wealthy and politically influential family. He was a distant cousin of Republican President Theodore Roosevelt. As a child, Roosevelt enjoyed all the advantages that money could provide: he had private tutors, went to prestigious private schools, and toured Europe with his family. He graduated from Harvard and studied law, but decided he wanted to make government service his career. He was elected to the New York state senate and served as secretary of the navy during World War I. In the election of 1920 Roosevelt was the Democratic vice-presidential candidate, but the ticket was defeated. He was a courageous fighter as was proven when, in 1921, polio crippled him for life. He refused to give up politics and was elected president 11 years later. The words he spoke at his inauguration, "The only thing we have to fear is fear itself," gave Americans confidence in his ability to lead. As president he had to deal with two of the biggest challenges in American history: The Great Depression and World War II. He implemented drastic reforms to help end the Great Depression and also led the nation through World War II. He died in office in 1945, just before the war ended and only about three months after the start of his fourth term.

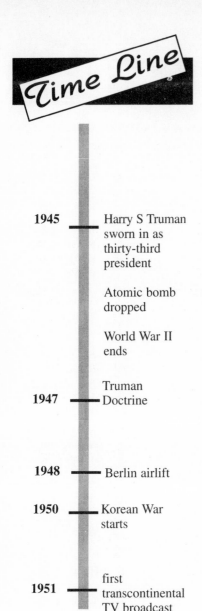

1945	Harry S Truman sworn in as thirty-third president
	Atomic bomb dropped
	World War II ends
1947	Truman Doctrine
1948	Berlin airlift
1950	Korean War starts
1951	first transcontinental TV broadcast

Harry S Truman

Courtesy Harry S Truman Library of Congress

Thirty-third President
Party: Democratic
Born: May 8, 1884—Lamar, Missouri
Died: December 26, 1972

Harry Truman was raised on the family farm. He never went to college. After high school, he had a variety of jobs. He wanted to go to the U.S. Military Academy at West Point, but his vision was too poor. His eyesight was good enough, however, to get into the state national guard and fight in Europe during World War I. After the war Truman returned to Missouri and opened up a small business and studied law. In 1934 he was elected to the U.S. Senate. He exposed corrupt political machines, and his investigation of defense spending saved the nation millions of dollars. He was nominated to be the Democratic vice-presidential candidate in the election of 1944. When President Franklin D. Roosevelt died at the start of his fourth term, Truman became president. Although unprepared for the presidency, Truman proved to be a strong leader. First, he had to deal with post-war Europe. He established the Truman Doctrine, which made it America's duty to stop the spread of communism. Truman also made the decision to drop the atomic bomb, which ended the war in the Pacific. He was elected to a full term in 1948 in an upset victory. Truman continued to lead the cold war fight against communism, establishing NATO to check the Soviet Union in Europe. He also supported the establishment of the United Nations.

Dwight D. Eisenhower

Courtesy Library of Congress

Time Line

1953	Dwight D. Eisenhower sworn in as thirty-fourth president
	Korean War armistice signed
1954	*Brown v. Board of Education* of Topeka
1955	Rosa Parks refuses to give up her seat on a bus to a white man
1957	First civil rights bill
	Little Rock High School resists desegregation
	Soviets launch *Sputnik,* world's first space satellite
1958	*Explorer I* first U.S. space satellite

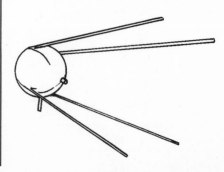

Thirty-fourth President
Party: Republican
Born: October 14, 1890—Denison, Texas
Died: March 28, 1969

Dwight D. Eisenhower grew up knowing what hard work and sacrifice were all about. He worked in his father's creamery to help pay for his brother's education. Eisenhower accepted an appointment to West Point and graduated from the military academy in 1915. During World War I, he trained tank battalions. Later, he served on General Douglas MacArthur's staff in the Philippines. During World War II, he commanded forces in North Africa and was appointed supreme commander of the Allied Expeditionary Force in Europe. He led the D-Day invasion in 1944. After the war he was a college president and commander of NATO. When it came time to pick a candidate for the election of 1952, the Republicans nominated Eisenhower. The popular war hero won by a landslide. During Eisenhower's term the cold war got even colder. Castro took over Cuba and established a communist government. The nation's confidence in itself was severely shaken when the Soviet Union launched *Sputnik,* the world's first space satellite. One of Eisenhower's greatest accomplishments was the construction of the interstate highway system. After completing two terms, Eisenhower retired to his farm in 1961.

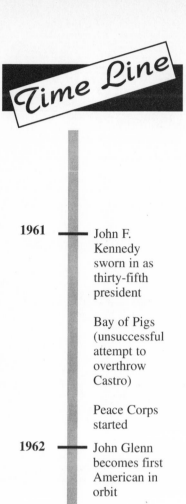

1961	John F. Kennedy sworn in as thirty-fifth president
	Bay of Pigs (unsuccessful attempt to overthrow Castro)
	Peace Corps started
1962	John Glenn becomes first American in orbit
	Cuban missile crisis
1963	March on Washington ("I Have a Dream" speech)
	Kennedy assassinated

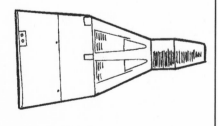

John F. Kennedy

Courtesy The White House

Thirty-fifth President
Party: Democratic
Born: May 29, 1917—Brookline, Massachusetts
Died: November 22, 1963

John F. Kennedy was born into a prominent, Irish-American family. His grandfather had been a politician, and his wealthy father had strong ties to the Democratic Party. After graduating from Harvard University, Kennedy joined the Navy. He captained a PT boat in the Pacific during World War II. Severely wounded in the war, he wrote a book, *Profiles in Courage,* while recovering in the hospital. The whole Kennedy family worked on his campaign when he ran for representative. He won, and his political career was launched. Kennedy was elected two more times to the House, and then he was elected to the U.S. Senate in 1952, and again in 1958. Kennedy projected an "image" on television that appealed to many voters. In the 1960 campaign Kennedy debated his opponent, Richard Nixon, on TV. His energetic and confident style helped him win. As president Kennedy started the Peace Corps, backed civil rights, and supported policies to halt the spread of communism. He enlarged the U.S. military role in Vietnam and stopped the installation of Soviet missiles in Cuba. Perhaps his greatest legacy was the national goal he set to landing a man on the moon before 1970. Kennedy did not live to witness that amazing achievement. In 1963 he was assassinated while riding in a motorcade in Dallas, Texas.

Lyndon B. Johnson

Courtesy Library of Congress

Thirty-sixth President
Party: Democratic
Born: August 27, 1908—Stonewall, Texas
Died: January 22, 1973

Lyndon B. Johnson graduated from Southwest Texas State Teachers College in 1930. He went to Washington to assist a member of the U.S. House of Representatives. In 1937 Johnson was elected to the House and served in that body for over ten years. He interrupted his political career to serve in the Navy during World War II. Johnson was elected to the U.S. Senate in 1948 and reelected in 1954. A hard-working and persuasive legislator, Johnson rose to the position of Senate majority leader. Johnson wanted the party to nominate him for president in 1960, but he was passed over in favor of John F. Kennedy. In a surprise move, Kennedy asked Johnson to be his running mate, and the two went on to win the general election. Johnson took the oath of office aboard *Air Force One* after Kennedy's assassination. He worked hard to hold the nation together and pass Kennedy's legislation. Johnson was elected to a full term in 1964. Johnson championed social reforms and pushed Congress to pass the landmark civil rights acts of 1964 and 1965. His Vietnam War policy, however, was a disaster. By 1968 the situation had become so unbearable that he withdrew from the presidential race and retired to his ranch in Texas.

Time Line

1963	Lyndon B. Johnson sworn in as thirty-sixth president
1964	Civil Rights Act
	Tonkin Gulf Resolution
	War on Poverty
1965	Malcolm X assassinated
	Selma March
	Voting Rights Act
	Medicare
1966	Bombing of Hanoi
1967	Twenty-fifth Amendment ratified
	Thurgood Marshall sworn in as first black U.S. Supreme Court justice
1968	Tet Offensive
	Martin Luther King, Jr., assassinated
	Robert Kennedy assassinated

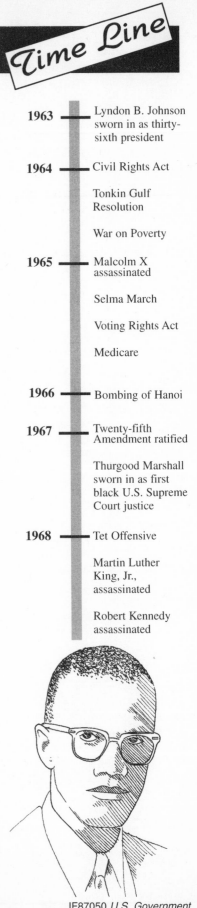

Time Line

1969 — Richard Nixon sworn in as thirty-seventh president

Withdrawal of U.S. troops from Vietnam begins

U.S. astronauts land on moon

1970 — Four student war protesters killed at Kent State

First Earth Day

1972 — Nixon goes to China

Nixon goes to Moscow

Strategic Arms Pact

Watergate break-in

1973 — *Roe v. Wade*

Vietnam Peace Agreement

Vice President Agnew resigns

Watergate cover-up

1974 — Nixon impeachment hearings

Nixon resigns presidency

Richard Nixon

Courtesy Library of Congress, Prints and Photographs Division [LC-USZ62-13037]

Thirty-seventh President
Party: Republican
Born: January 9, 1913—Yorba Linda, California
Died: April 22, 1994

Richard Nixon was raised in a middle-class family that valued hard work, patriotism, religion, and respect for education. He graduated from Duke University Law School in 1937. Nixon enlisted in the Navy during World War II. After the war, he was elected to the U.S. House of Representatives in 1946, and in 1950 he was elected to the U.S. Senate. In Congress Nixon became well-known as a member of a committee investigating communist activity within American society. While vice president, he was accused of misusing political donations, but he successfully defended himself in his famous "Checkers" speech. Nixon experienced his share of political defeats: he lost to Kennedy in 1960 and was defeated in his bid to become governor of California. However, he won the presidential election of 1968 and was reelected in 1972. He was successful in his policies toward China and the Soviet Union and took steps to end the Vietnam War. But a crisis at home drove him from office. Secret White House tapes revealed Nixon's role in a cover-up of a burglary into the Democratic Party headquarters in the Watergate building. As Congress moved to impeach him, Nixon resigned the presidency. A month later President Ford pardoned Nixon for any crimes he had committed while in office.

Gerald Ford

Courtesy Library of Congress, Prints and Photographs Division [LC-USZ62-13038]

Thirty-eighth President
Party: Republican
Born: July 14, 1913—Omaha, Nebraska
Died:

Born in Nebraska, Gerald Ford moved to Michigan when he was two years old. He liked school and was an excellent athlete. At the University of Michigan, Ford played on the football team. He graduated from Yale Law School in 1941 and began his law practice. When the United States entered World War II, he joined the Navy and fought in the Pacific. After the war he resumed his law practice and then decided to run for political office. He was elected to the U.S. House of Representatives. An extremely popular congressman, both among his colleagues in the House and the voters back home, Ford was elected to 13 terms and served as the minority whip. When Agnew resigned the vice presidency in 1973, Ford was nominated and approved to replace him. Then, eight months later, he became president when Richard Nixon was forced to resign because of the Watergate cover-up scandal. One of Ford's first and most controversial acts as president was to pardon Nixon. Ford tried to heal the nation, which was demoralized after Watergate and Vietnam. He also tried to deal with mounting economic ills. But as the Republican president and the Democrat-controlled Congress fought over what to do, conditions worsened. Despite Ford's gentle manner and good intentions, the public was not consoled. In the election of 1976 he lost his bid to become president in his own right.

Time Line

1974 — Gerald Ford sworn in as thirty-eighth president

Ford issues Nixon pardon

1975 — Americans evacuate Vietnam

1976 — Americans celebrate country's two-hundredth anniversary

Viking II lands on Mars

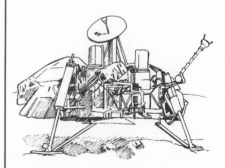

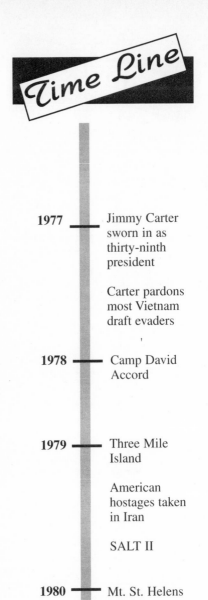

1977 — Jimmy Carter sworn in as thirty-ninth president

Carter pardons most Vietnam draft evaders

1978 — Camp David Accord

1979 — Three Mile Island

American hostages taken in Iran

SALT II

1980 — Mt. St. Helens erupts

Jimmy Carter

Courtesy Library of Congress, Prints and Photographs Division [LC-USZ62-13039]

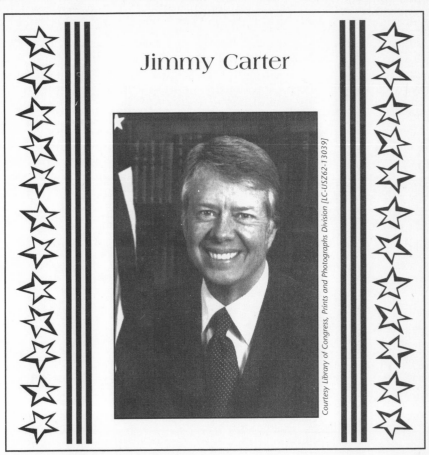

Thirty-ninth President
Party: Democratic
Born: October 1, 1924—Plains, Georgia
Died:

Jimmy Carter grew up in Plains, a small town in Georgia, where his family raised peanuts. A bright and diligent student, he gained an appointment to the U.S. Naval Academy and then served in the submarine program. When his father died, he resigned from the Navy and returned home to run the family business. He decided to enter politics and was elected state senator and then governor of Georgia. When Carter began campaigning for the presidency in 1976, he was virtually an unknown. But the country was ready for a change of leadership. Carter's call for a return of honest government appealed to voters. Unfortunately, after Carter's election, the economy got worse not better. There were oil shortages, price increases, and higher unemployment. In foreign affairs, Carter worked for peace. Thanks to his efforts, in 1978 the Israelis and Egyptians signed the Camp David Accord, an agreement to work for peace in the Middle East. In 1979 Carter reached an agreement, called SALT II, with the Soviet Union to limit nuclear weapons. Carter's greatest foreign policy dilemma occurred in 1979 when Americans were taken hostage by anti-U.S. militants in Iran. Carter's inability to obtain release of the hostages, along with the unsolved economic problems, contributed to his defeat in the election of 1980.

Ronald Reagan

Courtesy Library of Congress, Prints and Photographs Division [LC-USZ62-13039]

Fortieth President
Party: Republican
Born: February 6, 1911—Tampico, Illinois
Died:

Brought up in a family of modest means, Ronald Reagan worked to help pay his way through college, where he was active in theater and as a student leader. After college he was a sportscaster and then went to Hollywood and became a movie actor. He played in numerous movies and was also a spokesperson and actor on television. Reagan started out in politics as a Democrat but switched parties in 1962. As a Republican, he was elected governor of California twice. Reagan was a national leader of the conservative wing of the Republican Party. He supported business and hated communism. Extremely likeable and a gifted speaker, Reagan won the election of 1980 by a landslide and was reelected in 1984 in the greatest landslide in history. Reagan lowered taxes, which appealed to many Americans. But he also cut many social programs that helped the needy so that more money could be spent on the military. In 1981 he was wounded in an assassination attempt. In foreign policy Reagan and Soviet leader Gorbachev signed a pact to dismantle nuclear missiles. During Reagan's term, he battled international terrorism and supported anticommunist movements in Latin America. After retiring from office, Reagan told the nation he was suffering from Alzheimer's disease.

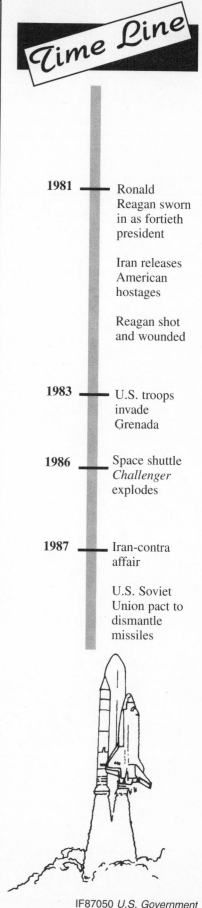

Time Line

1981 — Ronald Reagan sworn in as fortieth president

Iran releases American hostages

Reagan shot and wounded

1983 — U.S. troops invade Grenada

1986 — Space shuttle *Challenger* explodes

1987 — Iran-contra affair

U.S. Soviet Union pact to dismantle missiles

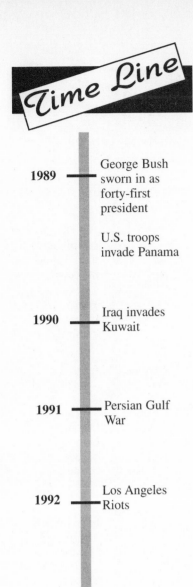

1989 — George Bush sworn in as forty-first president

U.S. troops invade Panama

1990 — Iraq invades Kuwait

1991 — Persian Gulf War

1992 — Los Angeles Riots

George Bush

Courtesy Library of Congress, Prints and Photographs Division [LC-USZ62-98302]

Forty-first President
Party: Republican
Born: June 12, 1924—Milton, Massachusetts
Died:

Born in New England into a well-to-do family, George Bush graduated from Yale University with a degree in economics. For two years Bush was a Navy pilot during World War II. He parachuted to safety when his plane was shot down in the Pacific. He won the Distinguished Flying Cross medal for his heroism. After the war Bush settled in Texas where he became a successful executive in the oil industry. Defeated in 1964 for a seat in the U.S. Senate, Bush later became the first Republican to represent Houston in the U.S. House of Representatives. He was reelected in 1968 without opposition. In 1970 Bush was defeated again in another try for the U.S. Senate. President Nixon appointed Bush to a number of high level government positions. He served as U.S. ambassador to the United Nations, chairman of the Republican National Committee, representative to China, and director of the CIA. After loyally serving two terms as vice president in the Reagan administration, Bush was elected president in 1988. During Bush's term, the cold war ended with the demise of communism and the breakup of the Soviet Union. Bush used American military power in Panama, and in 1991 he sent U.S. military forces to stop Iraq's invasion of Kuwait in the Persian Gulf War. A weak economy helped Bill Clinton keep Bush from achieving a second term.

William (Bill) Clinton

Courtesy Library of Congress, Prints and Photographs Division [LC-USZ62-107700]

Time Line

1993 — Bill Clinton sworn in as forty-second president

World Trade Center bombed

1994 — NAFTA

1995 — Oklahoma City bombing of federal building

1999 — Impeachment trial of Bill Clinton

Forty-second President
Party: Democratic
Born: August 19, 1946—Hope, Arkansas
Died:

Bill Clinton was raised in a small town in Arkansas. Bright and articulate, he did well in school. He graduated from Georgetown University and Yale Law School. Clinton also spent two years at Oxford University in Britain as a Rhodes Scholar. Returning to Arkansas, Clinton taught law and entered public service. In 1976 he was elected state attorney general and then was elected to five two-year terms as governor of Arkansas. While governor, Clinton earned a reputation as a reformer for his work in education. In 1992 Clinton was elected president and reelected in 1996. Early in his first term, Clinton wanted to radically reform health care but was unsuccessful. In foreign affairs, Clinton lobbied hard for Senate ratification of the North American Free Trade Agreement (NAFTA), which President Bush signed. In 1999 Clinton ordered U.S. military air strikes against Serbian forces in Kosovo, an area in southern Serbia, as part of a NATO action to stop ethnic killings. Clinton's presidency almost came to an end when he was impeached by the U.S. House of Representatives for lying about a relationship with a White House intern. The U.S. Senate failed to convict him of the charges.

2001 — George W. Bush sworn in as forty-third president

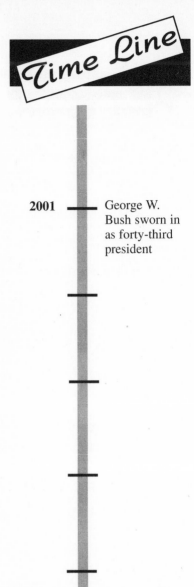

Highlight significant events in the Bush administration that have occurred up to the time of this assignment and add them to the time line.

George W. Bush

Forty-third President
Party: Republican
Born: July 6, 1946—New Haven, Connecticut
Died:

The son of former president George Bush, George W. Bush grew up in Texas, but went to prep school and college in New England. He was educated at Yale University and Harvard Business School. After college George W. returned to Texas and became a successful businessman. He was an owner of the Texas Rangers baseball team and when the team was sold, he was richly rewarded. In 1977 George W. launched his political career, running for a seat in Congress. Although he lost the election, he found out that he was a good campaigner. Many voters seemed attracted to his amiable personality and upbeat attitude. In 1994 George W. gained national recognition when he defeated popular incumbent Texas governor Ann Richards. Propelled by his reelection to a second term as governor of Texas, George W. Bush became the Republican Party's candidate in the presidential election of 2000. The Democrats chose Vice President Al Gore as their candidate. The election was so close that it took over a month to determine the winner. The struggle for the presidency came down to Florida. Both candidates needed Florida's 25 electoral votes to become president, but confusing ballots and questionable vote recounts made it difficult to determine the winner. The issue ended up in the U.S. Supreme Court, which decided in favor of George W. Bush.

Answer Key

Symbols of Our Nation
Page 5
1. E
2. F
3. J
4. D
5. C
6. B
7. H
8. I
9. G
10. A

In Your Own Words
Page 7
1. form a more perfect Union
2. establish Justice
3. insure Tranquility
4. provide for defense
5. promote general Welfare
6. secure Liberty

Steps Toward Revolution
Page 9
Answers are in order beginning from 1763 to 1775.
D, E, G, C, B, I, H, A, F

Framers of the Constitution
Page 11
1. Philadelphia
2. 55
3. half were lawyers and judges, one fourth were landowners, all had held one public office, and all were wealthy
4. to recommend changes in government
5. no, because they had different opinions about the best government
6. Franklin
7. Washington
8. Constitutional Convention
9. Madison
10. The new Constitution proposed a powerful executive and a Senate with powers equal to those of the House.

The Constitutional Convention
Page 12
Answers will vary.
Possible answers:
1. Probably favor New Jersey Plan because it would give your state the same number of representatives as states with large populations.
2. Probably favor Virginia Plan because it would give your state more representatives than states with smaller populations.
3. Might agree to the Connecticut Plan, which creates a two-house legislature. Someone from a state with a large population would probably be more inclined to agree than someone from a state with a small population.

Powerful Ideas
Page 13
1. E
2. G
3. I
4. B
5. D
6. H
7. C
8. A
9. F
10. J

Outlining the Constitution
Page 14
Article 1: Legislative branch
1. Legislative power
2. House
3. Senate
4. Elections and meetings
5. Legislative proceedings
6. Salaries, immunities & disabilities of members
7. Revenue bills; president's veto
8. Powers of Congress
9. Powers denied Congress
10. Powers denied states

Article II: Executive branch
1. Executive power, term, qualifications, salary, oath of office
2. President's powers
3. President's duties
4. Impeachment

Article III: Judicial branch

1. Judicial powers
2. Jurisdiction
3. Treason

Article IV: Relations of states
1. Full faith and credit
2. Privileges and immunities of citizens
3. New states and territories
4. Protection given states by the nation

Article V: Provisions for amendment

Article VI: Public debts, supremacy of national law, and oaths of office

Article VII: Ratification of Constitution

Amendments:
1. Freedom of speech, religion, press, assembly, and petition
2. Bearing arms
3. Quartering troops
4. Searches and seizures
5. Due process
6. Criminal proceedings
7. Civil trials
8. Punishment for crimes
9. Unenumerated rights
10. Powers reserved to states

Amendment Matchup
Page 15
A. 21st
B. 14th
C. 24th
D. 13th
E. 26th
F. 19th
G. 22nd
H. 17th
I. 25th
J. 15th
K. 20th
L. 18th
M. 23rd
N. 11th
O. 12th
P. 27th
Q. 16th

Constitution Fill-In
Page 16
1. Rhode Island
2. Nine
3. Confederation
4. president
5. Madison
6. House
7. Senate
8. executive
9. Philadelphia
10. Washington
11. First
12. women
13. judicial

The Civil Rights Amendments
Page 17

The Twenty-Sixth Amendment
Page 19
Answers will vary.
Possible answers:
1. The Twenty-sixth Amendment was ratified because Americans believed that anyone old enough to die in the military services in defense of his/her country was entitled to vote for the nation's leaders.
2. Possible reasons why voter turnouts among 18- to 24-year-olds is so low include apathy, alienation, and a sense that their votes will not make a difference or have an impact.
3.-4. Answers will vary.

Amending the Constitution
Page 20
1. V
2. Amendment; other answers will vary.

Organization of the U.S. Government — Page 21

1. E	10. J
2. J	11. E
3. L	12. L
4. E	13. L
5. L	14. J
6. L	15. L
7. J	16. E
8. E	17. J
9. E	18. L
	19. J

One Nation, Many Governments — Page 22

National: coining money; conduct foreign relations; raise an army; declare war
Shared: borrow money; power to tax; regulate voting **States:** education; roads; health and hospitals; law enforcement

Forms of Government — Page 23

1. In presidential powers are shared; in parliamentary power rests in the legislative branch.
2. In confederal each state is sovereign; in federal powers are shared between national and states, and in parliamentary the head of government is chosen from the ranks of the majority party.

A Federal System — Page 24

1. N	10. N
2. N	11. N
3. S	12. S
4. N	13. N
5. N	14. S
6. S	15. N
7. S	16. S
8. S	17. N
9. N	18. N

Branches of Government — Page 25

LEGISLATIVE BRANCH
impeach the president
pass laws over the president's veto by two-thirds majority vote of both houses
establish committees to oversee activities of executive branch
disapprove appointments made by the president
propose amendments to the U.S. Constitution

EXECUTIVE BRANCH
nominate members of the federal judiciary
veto laws passed by Congress

JUDICIAL BRANCH
overrule decisions made by lower courts
declare actions of the executive branch unconstitutional
declare laws made by Congress to be unconstitutional

Checks and Balances Chart — Page 26

Power	How It Can Be Checked		
	The President may	The Supreme Court may	Congress may
If Congress passes a law, then . . .	pass or veto it	declare the law unconstitutional	
If the president vetoes a bill passed by Congress, then . . .			override the veto with a 2/3 vote
If the president appoints a Supreme Court judge, then . .			the Senate may approve or disapprove the appointment
If a federal judge shows misconduct in office, then . . .			impeach the judge
If the president makes a treaty with another country, then . . .			the Senate may approve or disapprove the treaty
If the president enforces an unjust law, then . . .		declare the law unconstitutional	
If the president asks for money for defense, then . . .			or may not give it to the president

A Limited and Unlimited Government — Page 27

Limited: regular and free elections; independent judiciaries; protection of individual rights; protection from government; multiple political parties; laws apply to leaders as well as governed; goals and means of government cannot violate constitution; Great Britain; Canada; France
Unlimited: courts controlled by leader; no restraints on government; no free elections; government use of intimidation and terror; Soviet Union; Iraq; Libya; Italy under Mussolini; Myanmar; China

The Executive Branch — Page 28

1. 4 years
2. vice president
3. Born a citizen of the United States, at least 35 years old, have been a resident of United States at least 14 years.
4. The following should be checked: c, d, e, h, i.
5. See oath on page 31.

Cabinet Officers — Page 29

Check current source for names.

Presidential Power — Page 31

1. T	10. F
2. F	11. T
3. T	12. F
4. F	13. F
5. T	14. T
6. T	15. F
7. T	16. T
8. T	17. F
9. F	18. F

Presidency Fill-In — Page 32

1. chief executive	7. justices
2. enforce	8. White House
3. foreign	9. cabinet
4. defense	10. Congress
5. party	11. four
6. judicial	12. twice

The Electoral College — Page 33

1. T	7. F
2. T	8. T
3. F	9. T
4. T	10. T
5. T	11. F
6. T	12. T

The two presidents are Rutherford B. Hayes and Benjamin Harrison.

All About the House — Page 34

1. E	6. M
2. B	7. C
3. H	8. P
4. J	9. G
5. A	10. N

Senate Facts — Page 35

1. smaller	9. legislature
2. two	10. seventeenth
3. state	11. voters
4. 100	12. six
5. upper chamber	13. state
6. revenue bills	14. Constitution
7. treaties	15. president
8. appointments	16. tie
	17. pro tempore

Comparing Houses of Congress — Page 36

	Senate	House of Representatives
Number of members	100	435
How elected	by voters in state	by voters in district
Title of members	senator	representative
Constituents represented	whole state	district
Qualifications: age, citizenship, & residence	age 30, 9-yr. citizen, resident of state	age 25, 7-yr. citizen, resident of state
Length of term	6 years	2 years
Title of presiding officer	president	speaker of the House
Name of current presiding officer	Answers will vary.	Answers will vary.
Impeachment power	Senate convicts	House impeaches
Unique responsibilities	approves treaties and certain appointments	originates revenue bills

Making Laws — Page 37

A. 8
B. 6
C. 2
D. 3
E. 1
F. 4
G. 9
H. 5
I. 7

Impeachment — Page 38

1. chief justice
2. House
3. two-thirds
4. Congress
5. Senate
6. two
7. none

The President's name is Andrew Johnson

The Judicial Branch — Page 39

1. national
2. the Constitution
3. judicial
4. federal, state, local
5. justice

The Supreme Court — Page 40

Answers will vary.
1. In Gideon v. Wainwright (1963) the Supreme Court ruled that states must provide lawyers for defendants who cannot afford to hire their own lawyers.
2. In United States v. Wong Kim Ark (1898) the Supreme Court ruled that under the Fourteenth Amendment Wong was a native-born citizen of the United States.

Important Supreme Court Decisions — Page 41

1. E
2. I
3. F
4. B
5. D
6. C
7. A
8. J
9. G
10. H

Political Dictionary — Page 42

1. Q
2. F
3. O
4. A
5. D
6. E
7. M
8. L
9. B
10. H
11. J
12. I
13. G
14. C
15. K
16. N
17. P

Expressing Our Ideals — Page 46

1. C
2. F
3. G
4. A
5. D
6. B
7. E

A Citizenship Primer — Page 48

1. True
2. False, five years
3. False, does not need to read, write, and speak English
4. True
5. True

Rights and Responsibilities — Page 50

1. right
2. right
3. right
4. responsibility
5. right
6. right
7. right
8. right
9. responsibility
10. responsibility
11. responsibility
12. responsibility
13. responsibility
14. right
15. right
16. responsibility
17. right

Protecting Your Rights — Page 52

1. F
2. G
3. D
4. I
5. C
6. B
7. H
8. J
9. E
10. A

Wrongs and Rights — Page 53

1. C
2. F
3. B
4. D
5. H
6. I
7. E
8. A
9. G
10. J

Civil Disobedience — Page 54

Thoreau refused to pay his poll tax because he was opposed to slavery and the Mexican-American War.

Anthony helped organize the woman's suffrage movement. She was arrested for illegally voting in the 1872 presidential election.

King organized sit-ins, boycotts, andm arches to oppose segregation and discrimination.

Chavez organized boycotts of farm products.

Comparative Governments — Page 57

1. E
2. I
3. F
4. H
5. D
6. J
7. L
8. G
9. B
10. C
11. K
12. A

Becoming a Citizen — Page 71

2. Yes
3. By becoming a naturalized citizen by doing the following: be at least 18, live in the United States five years, be of good moral character, demonstrate knowledge of English, demonstrate knowledge of U.S. history and governement, and take an oath of allegiance.

Economic Decision-Making — Page 75

1. The U.S. government mark means that the food has been inspected and passed by the Department of Agriculture.

Answers for questions 2 through 7 will differ depending on the particular food label provided.

If You Could Vote Tomorrow — Page 78

Answers will vary.

Possible domestic issues include taxes, medicare, social security, education, crime, and the environment. Encourage students to research each issue they select before they prepare their writtten response.